CROSS-CULTURAL
SEMIOTIC DIALOGUES BETWEEN
CHINA AND THE WEST

中西跨文化符号学对话

郭景华 / 著

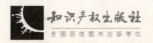
知识产权出版社
全国百佳图书出版单位

图书在版编目（CIP）数据

中西跨文化符号学对话 = Cross – cultural Semiotic Dialogues between China and the West：英文/郭景华著. —北京：知识产权出版社，2017.4

ISBN 978 – 7 – 5130 – 4851 – 4

Ⅰ.①中… Ⅱ.①郭… Ⅲ.①符号学—对比研究—中国、西方国家—英文 Ⅳ.①H0

中国版本图书馆 CIP 数据核字（2017）第 058057 号

内容提要

基于跨文化阐释多维模式，本书从书法、电影、小说、城市、戏剧等模态进行中西方文化符号对话，旨在向世界推介中国优秀文化，讲述好中国故事，传播好中国声音，为中华文化走出去寻找可行的海外传播途径。

责任编辑：兰　涛　　　　　　　　责任校对：王　岩

封面设计：郑　重　　　　　　　　责任出版：刘译文

中西跨文化符号学对话

Cross – cultural Semiotic Dialogues between China and the West

郭景华　著

出版发行：	知识产权出版社 有限责任公司	网　　址：	http：//www.ipph.cn
社　　址：	北京市海淀区气象路 50 号院	邮　　编：	100081
责编电话：	010 – 82000860 转 8325	责编邮箱：	lantao625@163.com
发行电话：	010 – 82000860 转 8101/8102	发行传真：	010 – 82000893/82005070/82000270
印　　刷：	三河市国英印务有限公司	经　　销：	各大网上书店、新华书店及相关专业书店
开　　本：	720mm×1000mm　1/16	印　　张：	12.5
版　　次：	2017 年 4 月第 1 版	印　　次：	2017 年 4 月第 1 次印刷
字　　数：	202 千字	定　　价：	38.00 元

ISBN 978 -7 -5130 -4851 -4

Acknowledgements

I am much indebted to Prof. Lopez – Varela for her professional guidance in writing this book, co-supervision for my Ph. D. at Beijing Language and Culture University, as well as a research stay at Universidad Complutense Madrid during the academic year 2014 – 2015. She is a welcome source of positive energy, encouraging me to continue my work during difficult times. I cannot adequately express how much I owe to her efforts. She is such an outstanding mentor and friend.

I also want to show my gratitude to Prof. Qing – ben Li, my Chinese doctoral tutor from Beijing Language and Culture University. During my doctoral studies, I have received a great deal of inspiration from his passion and devotion to his work. His personality and demeanor will remain an inspiration for me.

I also want to thank my parents and sisters. Their concern and care for me are an immense comfort. Whenever I would slip into an occasional melancholy mood, they would fill my life with delicious meals and loving smiles. Their efforts would always result in the return of my strength and positive attitude.

Finally I want to express my sincere thanks to my husband, Yan Shi and son, Yan Zihan. They have always given me their full support and selfless love during these years. Without their support and encouragement I could not have completed my goals or pursue my academic endeavors. Because of them, my world is always warm and full of sunshine.

FORWORD

The object of the research is the study of cross – cultural patterns between the People's Republic of China and the West. Here, culture is understood not just as "symbolic" (Burke, 1941) but, rather, as "semiotic action", in the Peircean sense of the word. That is, culture is, above all, and as Clifford Geertz has pointed out in *The Interpretation of Culture* (1973), human behavior that might take the form of phonation in speech, pigment in painting, line in writing, sound in music, texture in sculpture, form in architecture, and so on. In other words, culture signifies, and it does no matter if it is understood in cognitive terms, as a frame of mind, or in a more pragmatic sense, as patterned conduct.

Both Kenneth Burke and Clifford Geertz have argued that as a symbolic system, it is possible to isolate cultural elements, specify their internal relationships and characterize the entire system according to the core symbols around which is organized, capturing the underlying structures of which culture is a surface expression, and the ideological principles upon which it is based, explains Geertz. But as this anthropologist warns, the hermeneutical approach to the study of culture runs the risk of locking cultural analysis away from its object, which is human social life itself.

This research seeks to attend to culture not just as a "system of signs" (Lotman, Uspensky Mihaychuk, 1978: 211), but as "semiotic action" by showing concrete forms of behavior in which cultural forms find articulation. These forms can range from objects to states of consciousness (ideas, values, feelings, and so on). The important thing to bear in mind is that they "signify", and that they do so by drawing their meaning from the social role they play in a given society, or in Ludwig Wittgenstein's terms from their "use" in the system of relationships that is life. In this sense, cultural models are not just semantic, borrowing their capacity to signify from the sphere of natural languages. Yuri Lotman produced several interesting contributions to the study of cultural semiotics. One of such is the conception of "modelling system" as a structure of elements and of rules for combining them that is in a state of fixed analogy to the entire sphere of an object of knowledge, insight or regulation. Therefore a modeling system can be regarded as a language. Systems that have a natural language as their basis and that acquire supplementary superstructures, thus creating languages of a second level, can appropriately be called secondary modeling system. Thus, natural language is posited as the primary, or basic, infrastructure for all other human sign systems. In 1971 Lotman and Uspenski (in English 1978) elaborated their view of the semiotic study of culture, noting that, in their scheme, language is viewed as carrying out a specific communicative function by providing the collective with a presumption of communicability. Semiosis is also influenced by the habitus, i. e., by the semi – conscious dispositions that people, particularly in their early lives, acquire through social/material interaction with their habitat and through the social relations in their part of the social field (Bourdieu, 2000). Norman Fairclough, Bob Jessop and Andrew Sayer (2001) have argued that:

> There are three sets of semiotic conditions of existence of the reproduction and the transformation of social structures, institutions, etc. First, there are the conditions of existence of the reproduction and transformation of social groups, organizations, institutions, and other social phenomena. These concern, interalia, the variation, selection, and retention of their various features. It is important to note, second, that these conditions include the variation, selection and retention of their semiotic features. And, third, the conditions of existence of the variation, selection and retention of these various features of social phenomena generally include semiotic as well as other conditions of existence. In other words, semiosis itself can generate variation, have selective effects, and contribute to the differen-

tial retention and/or institutionalisation of social phenomena. (2001: 10)

The authors point out that the semiotic conditions of existence of the varia-tion, selection and retention of features favouring the reproduction of any social phenomenon comprise:

a) The selection of particular discourses for interpreting events, legitimising actions, and representing social phenomena. Semiotic factors operate here by inf luencing the differential (hegemonic) resonance of discourses.

b) The enactment of these selected discourses (positioned ways of represen-ting social practices) as ways of acting, both semiotically [in genres, that is, ways of regulating (inter) action; i. e an interview] and non – semiotically (e. g. , in organizational procedures).

c) The inculcation of these discourses in the ways of being/ identities of so-cial agents both semiotically (e. g. , ways of talking) and somatically (bodily dispositions).

d) The objectification of these discourses in the built environment, techno-logy, etc. , in organizational practices, and in the body/bodies.

e) The development of filtering devices within procedures for selecting these discourses, filtering out or legitimizing others.

f) The selection of strategies for agents (strategies for acting and for inter-preting) which privilege these discourses (discourses may become enacted as genres and inculcated as styles).

g) The resonance of these discourses (genres, styles, strategies) within the broader ensemble of social phenomena, as well as their complementarity with others within the network.

h) The capacity of the relevant social groups, organizations, institutions, etc. , to selectively "recruit" and retain social agents whose predispositions fit maximally with requirements. (Summary from Fairclough, Jessop and Sayer 2001: 10 – 11)

From the above, it is clear that culture is not just a static repository of the historical memory of a community, selecting those events to remember and those facts to forget. In determining the limits of memory, culture becomes a dynamic generator of acts of signification; acts that are presented not only as an aggregate of texts (normative and canonical or not), but as a repository that includes multimodal forms of culture, such as images, sounds, textures and so on. Any physical activity, material artefact or technology has the potential and "affordance" (potential uses of a given object; Gibson, 1976) of constituting itself in a semiotic system and, thus, in a signifying cultural resource. The term "semiotic resource" originates in the work of Michael Alexander Kirkwood Halliday (1978: 192) who extended Jakobson's notion of "code" to include not just communicative actions but also the artefacts we use to communicate (see chapter two for an extended discussion).

Because culture is always national, but also always international and transnational, this research focuses on the study of how these "semiotic actions" transcend the specificity of a given nation, in this case, the People's Republic of China. There are at least two ways by which the national can become international: translation and cross-cultural interpretation. Translation covers not only the conversion of language, but also cultural variations which are not just unidirectional but multidirectional, that is, cultural intersections take place across space and time (Li and Guo, "Rethinking the Relationship..." 45 - 60). The history and memory of a nation, its literary works, and other records in print form can be passed on and translated across space and also across time. These records can offer insights into the symbolic dimensions of the social actions of a given nation, its art, ideology, religion, laws, morality, science, technology. They function as sign - systems that contain information that can function as "templates" for the organization of the individual and the social, as Geertz explains in "Ideology as a cultural system". Interestingly, he indicates that they come most crucially into play in situations where the particular kind of information they contain is lacking, and where guides of behavior, thought or feeling are weak or absent, in other words, in a foreign environment. As he poetically puts it "It is in country unfamiliar emotionally or topographically that one needs poems and road maps".

It is for this reason that the present research on cross –cultural communication takes as its main focus the study of works of art as cultural objects, and it does so contemplating them in various forms and formats, from the printed literary text to the painted image and digitalized intermedial forms of e–literature. Creative art provides not merely criticism and answers for given social situations. Again, as Geertz suggests, imaginative works are strategic and intuitive cultural roadmaps, often foretelling and looking ahead as they contemplate the present and the past. In this sense, the artistic works under study in this research are "strategies" that, as Geertz indicates, sum up cultural situations, considering their structure and characteristics, and providing them with meaning (Geertz uses the word "naming" them) in a way that contains an attitude towards them. In other words, art not only provides cultural meaning, it does so by preserving important states emotional states of mind. Although representations, and therefore somehow fictions, this conception of the artwork as a strategy for handling public cultural content deals with situations that are "real" . And as Geertz adds, in so far as situations overlap from individual to individual, or from one historical period to another, the strategies possess universal relevance, that is, they may become cross – cultural.

In order to understand the above, we need to approach the artwork as a "strategy" for the representation of cultural situations from a multidimensional position that includes the creator, the material format which contains the concept⁄ idea, the dissemination strategies used to transfer the artistic content, and the audiences who receive it. Thus, methodologically, this research uses semiotic approach that deals with signs both intra – systematically and inter – systematically, as Umberto Eco (1985) has pointed out. In order to reach the cultural and the cross – cultural we need a semiotic system that deals with signs in the widest possible sense, to be sure, including the linguistic sign, but not only. The flexibility of Eco's definition applied to this research enables us to establish semiotics as an interdisciplinary master code. The semiotic frame will strengthen the process of reorganizing the methodological network across different historical and geographic cultural topographies.

This approach allows us to study messages transmitted in diverse ways, including new technologies. For centuries, communities have developed simple tools for communication, from drums to smoke signals to written messages on stones and other objects. Animals, like pigeons, were also used to carry messages across larger distances. Marshal McLuhan (1964) claimed that the type of technology developed to record and transmit messages determines how people process and remember them. Any major change in how information is represented and transmitted brings about a concomitant paradigm shift in cultural systems. He mentions the development of cuneiform writing from stones to clay tablets and its adaptation to papyrus and in hieroglyphic and later alphabetic forms, which made possible the advance of Greek cities (polis) and the advance of laws (from pol is > politics) in the Greco – Roman empire. In the Middle – ages, the printing press facilitated the dissemination of knowledge broadly and widely. In the 20th – century, radio and television reached millions of homes all over the world, paving the way for the Internet revolution of the 1990s which connected the entire world in what McLuhan called the "global village".

Culture is about both, the transmission of information and communication, including messages that carry not just conscious knowledge but also unconscious and emotional content, such as values, ethical and religious views, aesthetic imprint (what is good or bad related to what is beautiful or ugly), and so on. For this reason, it is important to revise how cross – cultural communication is possible by means of representational objects that change, as human communication formats evolve.

These changes in communication formats can be contemplated in terms of forms of semiotic translation. For example, in *intersemiotic* translation, one or more channels of communication used in the translated text differ (s) from the channel (s) used in the original text. In other words, the source and target text are semiotically non – equivalent. In *intrasemiotic* translation, the sign systems used in source and target text are identical, a case of semiotic equivalence. Whereas "intersemiotic translation" is a notion directly borrowed from Roman Jakobson (1959), the term "intrasemiotic translation" is used here as an umbrella term for Jakobson's "interlingual" and "intralingual" types of translation.

In this research, the emphasis on semiotics an indication of a general research orientation which is first characterized by its strong interdisciplinary strategy, as it accepts numerous theoretical tools from various disciplines in terms of a new methodological framework. Furthermore, it deals with various semantic le-vels ranging from the linguistic, communicative, pragmatic, expressive, and rhetoric at various levels of inter – artistic exchanges. Such a multi-semantic-layered semiotics can provide comparative scholars with the theoretical tools to more precisely analyze divergent cultural manifestations.

The cross-cultural paradigm I propose is also based upon constructionist tenets, and contemplates several levels of syntagmatic and paradigmatic analysis and interpretative scales within culture. The studies to be presented in the following pages offer successive re-interpretations and translations, in the wide sense of the word, that show the complex multidimensional patterns present in culture, and that suggest that global identity is the result of a dialogue between territories; a dialogue performed by means of semiotic interchanges present in cultural products that were exchanged across nations. I shall focus on a range of these cultural products, including texts, images, firm and theatre, as well as contemporary forms of digital culture.

Various chapters in this research deal with different forms of inter and intra semiotic translation. The particularities of Chinese culture and thought can be first seen expressed in the semiotic organization of its communication systems, namely, in what refers to writing, its character-centrist writing system. This system holds that form of writing is prior to that of sound and meaning. A single written unit (character) can be correspondent to several or numerous sounds and their related meanings almost in an irregular way. In its pictographic origin, a character kept an imagistic constancy because of a stability of the sketchy structure of the basic strokes of the character. Thus, one written character is not the representative of one idea or concept; instead it can be the sign for different ideas. This structure of one – visual – sign vs. Multiple meanings is very different from the Western sound – conceptual correspondent pattern, and it reveals the Daoist and Confucian elements made present in Chinese culture in the use of written signs. Thus, a character can be used by different people to express different things and signify different meanings in a flexible way. This does not mean that the same character does not maintain a conceptual unit and that it refers to multiple categories. Rather, it means that it has different uses. As You-Zheng Li (2001) has argued in his paper on "Chinese Philosophy and Semiotics" Chinese philosophical concepts exist neither in a logical hierarchy nor in a semantic consistence. In fact, we can hardly trace back to a conceptual lineage of a character-word. Furthermore, the combinational possibilities of Chinese characters are emphasized by the use of flexible elements that increase connotation, functioning at the emotional, volitional, rhetoric and other layers. A character can present several meanings, depending on the semic elements that conform it. After the transition from the earlier single – character concept system to the modern two – character one, the intersection of two *seme*-sets has contributed to restrict and define meaning, which was more vague and pluralistic when the single – character was used in classical texts. Thus, as You – Zheng Li indicated, the one – character concept system based on the Chinese written – character system established a special argumentative rhetoric characterized by its multi-semic-layer vocabulary and signification, including levels of logic as well as emotion and aesthetic converging on the same character word.

From the point of view of semiotics, when translating Chinese Classics, discourse is reformulated according to the stricter logical standards used in Western languages and though, in a way that other important semantic layers lose effect or are suppressed. Thus, although direct translation from Chinese to Western language leaves out various layers of meaning, the reverse process is even more difficult, as Western languages are unable to capture the multisemic potentialities of

Chinese. Qingben Li (2015) has demonstrated that a serious problem occurs when comparatists translate traditional Chinese texts from a Western centrist framework, placing emphasis on the logic aspects of meaning and leaving aside all other Chinese coloring. The translated texts convey only a partial message of the original. This semantic loss is not caused by translators' insufficient understanding of the original texts. Rather, it is the result of natural barriers with regards to semantic organization.

From the point of semiotics, the multi – dimensional interpretation of the one – character concept in traditional Chinese texts would indicate perhaps, as You – zheng Li (2001) has suggested, a weaker capability in organizing logical reasoning in texts. Besides, the direction of connotation in these texts pointed towards the emotional/moral side, with a strong pragmatic component, not just in Confucianism, but also in the other schools of thought that spread all over China. This would also mean a reduce level of scientific reasoning, argues Li. Similarly, in their quasi – philosophical discourse Chinese did not attempt a systematic construction of their verbal argumentation, let alone conceptual definition, rules of logical and causal inference, and categorical hierarchy. As evidence, You-Zheng Li points out the pictoriographic origin of Chinese character-words.

The first chapter of this research deals with the differences between semiology and semiotics, both English terms deriving from the Greek *semeîon* or "sign", which seek to investigate and understand the nature of signs and the laws governing them in the West. The second chapter explores the relationship between language, thought and cultural processes along the lines just suggested. For instance, the one – character concepts in the *Book of Changes* do not define each other in a rational way. Their logic operative sequences are not just given by the authors of the book, but by later interpreters, such as Confucian and Daoist scholars. Each character—concept, *Dao* (way), *Tien* (heaven), and so on, contains a history of the notional development and uses of that character. Different semantic parts of the character would play a more important role depending on the context. Thus, Chapter three traces the roots of the peculiar characteristics Chinese semiotics in ancient philosophical texts and in contemporary ones, and Chapter four studies the origins of Chinese writing and calligraphy. This chapter shows how a name category like *Tian* ☯ carries visual associations that are transferred to its different semic sets in a flexible way, thus carrying different notional implications, interpreted differently, for instance, the the Confucian and Daoist schools of thought, and later in contemporary Neo – Confucionism. Another example is the ideogram for *Ren* is a composite of 人 (Man, a man, a person) and 二 (two), where 人, as mentioned, assumes its form inside another character, to which various interpretations have been assigned. In other words, it operates as a causal "index", using Charles S. Peirce's terminology. *Ren* is generally translated as Benevolence, the most important concept in Confucian thought. Its iconography suggests the relation and equal treatment between two people. Examples of the inter – semiotic aspects of Chinese calligraphy are further explored in Chapter 4, which the following chapter expands to the area of Chinese and Mongolian Heritage. Chapter six presents the multidimensional cross – cultural paradigm that informs this research and which based on complex spatiotemporal patterns justified by the previous semiotic arguments. Chapter seven offers an example applied to both inter and intra – lingual semiotic translation. This is followed by an exploration of the semiotics of the city of China Hong Kong as a multicultural enclave.

REFERENCES

[1] Fairclough Norman, Bob Jessop and Andrew Sayer. Critical Realism and Semiosis [D] Paper presented at the International Association for Critical Realism Annual Conference, Roskilde, Denmark, 17–19th August 2001. http: //www. criticalrealism. com/archive/iacr_ conference_ 2001/nfairclough_ scsrt. pdf

[2] Fairclough Norman. Analysing Discourse: Textual Analysis for Social Research [M] . London and New York: Routledge, 2003.

[3] Fairclough Norman and Wodak, R. Critical discourse analysis. [M] // T. A. van Dijk

(Ed.). 1997. Discourse as Social Interaction. London and New Delhi: Sage, 1997: 285 – 284.

[4] Geertz Clifford. The Interpretation of Culture [M] . NY: Basic Books, 1973.

[5] Jakobson R. and M. Halle. Fundamentals of Language [M] . The Hague: Mouton de Gruyter, 1956.

[6] Jakobson Roman. Coup d'oeil sur le devéloppement de la sémiotique [M] //Panorama Sémiotique/A Semiotic Landscape. Ed. Seymour Chatman, Umberto Eco, and Jean – Marie Klinkenberg. Proceedings of the International Association for Semiotic Studies, Milan, June 1974; The Hague: Mouton de Gruyter, 1979: 3 – 18.

[7] Li Qingben. Intersemiotic Translation: Zen and Somaesthetics in Wáng Wéi's poem "Dwelling in Mountain and Autumn Twilight" [M] //López – Varela, A. & Ananta Sukla (Eds.) . The Ekphrastic Turn: Inter – Art Dialogues. New Directions in the Humanities book series. Champaign, University of Illinois Research Park, USA: Common Ground Publishing, 2015.

[8] Li Youzheng. Chinese Philosophy and Semiotics [M] //Two Roads to Wisdom: Chinese and Analytic Philosophical Tradition. Chicago: Bo Mou, Open Court, 2001.

[9] Li Youzheng. On the semic structure of traditional Chinese Philosophical words [M] // Historiography Quarterly, 1997 (4).

[10] Lotman Yuri, Uspensky B. A. , Mihaychuk George. On the Semiotic Mechanism of Culture [J] . New Literary History1978 (9): 211 – 232. Baltimore: The Johns Hopkins University Press. URL: http: //www. jstor. org/stable/468571.

[11] Lotman Yuri. Primary and Secondary Communication Modeling Systems [M] //P. Lucid. Soviet Semiotics. Baltimore: The Johns Hopkins University Press, 1977: 95 – 98.

Contents

Chapter 1

The Origins of Western
Semiotics and Its Evolution

According to Tzvetan Todorov (1977: 15 – 31; Charles William Morris, 1946: 335), four traditions have contributed to the "birth of Western semiotics", semantics (including the philosophy of language), logic, rhetoric and hermeneutics. There is, however, a much older tradition of implicitly se-miotic studies concerned with the nature of signs and communication. As an interdisciplinary/cross – cultural approach, semiotics also involves a comparative strategical shift, encompassing academic attitudes that examine the points of contact and divergence among cultural traditions, breaking up the traditional comparatist geographic – historical distinction, and supporting the multi – dimensional cross-cultural paradigm for exchanges between East and West presented in this volume.

The etymology of semiotics is related to the Greek words σήμεῖον "sign" and σμα "signal, sign". The related roots semio – (the Latinized transliteration of the Greek form semeio – , sema – and seman – have been the basis for the derivation of various terms in the field of semiotics and semantics. The major rival to the term semiotics has been semiology. For some time, these two terms used to be identified with the "two traditions" of semiotics (Sebeok, 1979: 63). The linguistic tradition, which originated from Ferdinand de Saussure (1857 – 1913) and was termed "semiology", and the general theory of signs in the tradition of Charles S. Peirce (1839 – 1914) called "semiotics". Today, semiotics is generally accepted either as a synonym of semiology or as a more general term, which includes semiology as one of its branches. Below I describe the two traditions in more detail.

In a very interesting article on the origin of the term semiotics, Wenceslao Castañares describes the use of the first terms related to the *sem* – family. He explains how both *sêma* and *semaínein* appear in Homer, in two senses "tomb", and "signal". *Semaínein* is also frequently used in the sense of "to give an order" and consequently, the person who gives orders (chief, charioteer, etc.) is named *sêmántor* (*Il.* , VIII, 127; *Od.* , XVII, 21 cited in Castañares, 2013: 14). Hesiod utilizes *sêma* very similarly. *Semeîon* appears in Aeschylus, Aesop, Hecataeus of Miletus, Anaxagoras, Cleostratus, etc. Aeschylus puts into use this term to refer to the emblems warriors wore engraved on their shields (*Seven against Thebes*, 397 – 398, 591, 643 cited in Castañares, 2012: 14). On other occasions, we could understand it as an "indication" (*Agam.* , 1355 cited in Castañares, 2012: 15), even as a "proof" (*Prom. Bound*, 842). In Sophocles, something similar happens: *semeîon* is used in the sense of "indication" (*Antig.* 257, 998 cited in Castañares, 2012: 15) or "proof" (*Oed. Tyr.* , 710 cited in Castañares, 2012: 15).

Similarly, *símbolon* meant to join and bring together, and was later employed as a sign of identity, and in the course of time, as a secret sign. Writers of the late sixth and the early fifth centuries BC, like Aeschylus, already resort to it in the sense of a conventional sign. Thereby, for instance, it is found in his tragedy *Agamemnon*, pointing to the light from torches, which is interpreted as a sign that somebody arrives with news (*Agam.* , 8 cited in Castañares, 2012: 16), or as an agreed sign serving to transmit quickly the piece of news that Troy has been conquered (*Agam.* , 315 cited in Castañares, 2013: 16). In Euripides (*Med.* , 614 cited in Castañares, 2012: 16), we can find it as a sign of recognition. Additionally we spot it in the same author as a secretly agreed sign (*Helen*, 291 cited in Castañares, 2012: 16), acceptation that, very much later, already in our era, will be found in Plutarch (*Cons. ad uxor.* , 611D 8, Goodwin, 1874: 10 cited in Castañares, 2012: 16), suggesting the mystic symbols of the orgiastic Dionysian rites. The above mentioned sense of conventional sign is maintained in the classical age. The way in which Plato uses it in *The Symposium* is particularly significant when narrating the myth according to which men were originally spherical (189d ff.). In Aristotle, the traditionally acquired sense is already found: that of a conventional, cultural sign whose paradigm is the word. This will be the sense handed down to the Western Christian tradition.

These terms also appear in relation to Greek medical science in the 5th century BCE when Hippocrates and his disciples described themselves as driven by observation, indications, conjectures and proofs. In the 2nd century CE, the physician Galen of Pergamum (139 – 199) , referred to diagnosis as a process of semesiosis (σημείωσις). To Galen, illness manifests itself through symptoms (*symptómata*) which must be evaluated as signs (*semeîa*) that is, allowing the knowledge through the observable evidence. The sign is defined as that which, once apprehended, permits to know something previously unknown. It is said that "semiosis" (*semeíosis*) is the form or appearance (*eídos*) of the sign and yet, that it is the grasping or knowledge (*katálepsis*) obtained through the sign, what the sign makes visible (*delotikón*) from something invisible (*ádelou*) (Galen, XIX 394, 16 K cited in Castañares, 2012: 22).

Plato

The recording of information in memory has been at the center of Western philosophical discourse at least since Plato (c. 428 – 347 BCE). If innate ideas constitute a sort of ontological memory, recoverable through anamnesis, signs are only shadows of shadows and what is learned and remembered through sensorial experience can only be accidental and superficial and not lead to the absolute truth (the world of Ideas). However, Plato's belief in the immaterial world of Ideas should not be interpreted as a negation of signs and languages. To get to close to Truth, human can use signs (sounds, words, drawing of images). Although the Forms of the world are ephemeral and change with time (i. e. the phonetics of words changes from person to person) there a certain correspondence that serves as a bridge with the world of Ideas. Plato's explanation appears in the myth of the cavern in Book VII of *The Republic*, where he compares perception to a man sitting in a cave looking at a wall and seeing only the shadows reflected from the real things behind his back outside the cave where the light is.

Plato's fundamental contribution appears undoubtedly in the *Cratylus*, where the conversation Socrates keeps with his two interlocutors, Hermogenes and Cratylus, is not focused on the nature of language or on language functions in general, neither on its origin; not even on the naturalness or conventionality of names, but on the accuracy or "correctness of names" to designate that which they represent. Hermogenes urged Socrates to accept that "whatever name you give to a thing is its right name; and if you give up that name and change it for another, the later name is no less correct than the earlier, just as we change the name of our servants, for I think no name belongs to a particular thing by nature" (Harris, 1987: 67).

In semiotic terms, we would say nowadays that the name is more an index than a symbol (in Peirce's terms). And it is only from this perspective that the etymological discussion extending over a great part of the dialogue gains sense. But there is an underlying and, if anything, a more radical problem: if the access to truth through the word is possible. The examination of Platonic texts drives us to the conclusion that the answer to this question is negative, so that the search for a universal language system has been maintained until the 21st century, in the work of Noah Chomsky for instance.

Plato's semiotics may be summarized as follows: (1) Verbal signs, whether natural or conventional, are only incomplete representations of the true nature of things. (2) The study of words reveals nothing about the true nature of things since the realm of ideas is independent of its representation in the form of words. (3) Knowledge mediated by signs is indirect and inferior to immediate knowledge, and truth about things through words, even if words are excellent likenesses, is inferior to knowing the truth itself (Coseriu, 1970: 58 –59).

Plato's position was a particular instance of what later came to be known as realism. According to him, the names of things a Forms that refer to the existence of universal abstract Ideas. A name, according to Plato, is not a mental entity or an idea in the mind of a person formed as a result of his having seen many concrete tables, rather it is an unchanging universal or an immortal Idea that exists independently of space and time. This raises the question of how are abstract universals or general ideas related to concrete things or specific objects of the experiential world. In other words, how is knowledge possible (this is known in philosophy as "epistemology").

The concept of mimesis

It is also important to explore the concept of mimesis, as it originates in Plato and later in his successor Aristotle. One important goal of theories of art is to distinguish between art and non-art. An art theory, sometimes condensed into a definition of art, should help us to understand what art is, how it works, and how it differs from other human activities and artifacts. In most handbooks, it is maintained that the theory of imitation (*mimesis*) is one of the major art theories in the West. The theory of imitation as we find it in ancient texts is not, however, a theory of art; it is a theory of pictorial representation. The ancient theory of imitation was never used to distinguish between fine arts and their products and other human skills and artifacts. The basic distinction for the ancient theory of imitation was that between pictures and real things. As Plato maintains in *The Sophist*, the imitation is a sort of "man – made dream produced for those who are awake" (266 C). This idea was, however, rejected by most critics, considered inadequate and superficial.

One of the first to suggest that aesthetics was an intellectual pursuit was Alexander Baumgarten (1714 – 1762). He distinguished between what we receive from our sense and what we think, claiming that aesthetics was concerned with sensuous knowledge, as logic was concerned with thought. Among the forms of mental images, aisthesis was described in the ancient tradition as the process in which mental images of the contingent qualities of individual things are presented to the mind. The basic metaphor used to characterize this process was that of pressure. An individual thing presses its contingent qualities upon the senses as if stamped into wax or a clay writing tablet. The class of mental images was divided into serveral subclasses that were distinguished from each other with regard to vividness, consistency, and relation to the outside world. Traditionally, six different mental occurrences were regarded as mental images of individual things. (*Correct*) *perceptions* of things in the world are true to the things perceived and are also vivid and consistent. Distorted images are *illusions. Hallucinations* were described as mental images caused by fever, drugs, etc. , with no relation, neither true nor distorted, to objects in the outside world. Their vividness and consistency may vary. The three types, perceptions, illusions and hallucinations are received by or generated within the person having them, and this reception has often been seen as a passive process. *Memories* are another type of such images. When we remember something we have a mental image of that something, and we know that the mental image does not now answer to something. in the world, but that it has done so. *Dreams* are another kind of mental image generated by the mind or the sensory apparatus. Dreams are sometimes very lively but seldom consistent, and a dream has no correct relation to the outside world in the sense of being an image of a particular external and existing object. Occasionally, elements in the dream can refer to particular existing thing, but that is not characteristic of them. Dreams are, instead, characterized by their ability to freely combine previously experienced material. Finally, *imaginations* are another kind of mental image, created by the senses without answer to something in the outside world. Like memories, but unlike "passive mental images", imaginations can be generated by will, at least to some degree.

When Plato calls imitations, "man made dreams produced by those who are awake," he singles out the apprehension of pictures as yet another distinct kind of mental image. Looking at or listening to an imitation resembles a dream, but it is not a dream because the spectator is awake. This fact implies that the viewer or listener is aware that it is an imitation and not a real thing which he or she is apprehending. The possibility of perceptual mistakes when looking at or listening to imitations was of great concern to Plato. In the *Sophist* (268 BCE), he characterizes sophists as imitators, he sees them as having an outward behaviour similar to that of wise men. In reality, however, they are not wise, they just appear to be wise, and that is all they intend. Plato seems to fear that most people are tricked by such illusions, a concern he expresses in the *Republic* (595B). Pictures (*eidolon*) and imitations are man – made as distinguished from reflections and shadows, which are made by nature and the creator (*Sophist*, 265B – 266D). The real danger for Plato is the moral influence exerted on human behaviour by these imitations. In his *Ars Poetica* (1 – 37), Horace adds that the imitation must also show a degree of ethical *decorum*.

Similarity is in ancient thought understood as having properties in common and the idea that individual things and mental images can have properties in common was founded in the belief that perception basically is a kind of impression, a process in which individual objects deliver their shapes but not their matter to the mind. Thus, the mental image as a kind of individual impression issimilar to the external individual object, it represents by having properties in common with it within the range of the capacity of the relevant sense organ. Imitations and pictures are things seen or heard, and the properties they can share with the things they represent must therefore be capable of being seen or heard. Furthermore, a picture or an imitation cannot share all of the properties of the thing represented. If something shares all of the properties of something else, it is not a picture or imitation of that thing but a second example of it (*Cratylus*, 432 A – B). The fact that an imitation is only partially similar to the thing it represents may help the viewer classify the thing he is apprehending as an imitation and not a real thing. Finally, the only function of a picture and an imitation is to be similar to a certain extent to the thing represented (*Sophist*, 240 B).

Aristotle

The relative significance of ontological and epistemology was explored by Plato's successor, Aristotle (384 – 322 BCE), who attempted to explain the relationship between the objects of the world (referents) and the signs we use to speak about them in his work *Peri Hermeneias* (in Latin *De Interpretatione*), the second book of his *Organon*. Aristotle's *De Interpretatione* address the elements compounding the statements, the name and the verb, as well as the affirmation and denial, basic constituents around which Aristotle will cultivate his theory on relationships of logical opposition among statements. It is, apart from that, the f irst explicit exposition about the breaking of the link between words and things (the *lógos* and the *ón*). Here we have a first version of the famous "triangle" in whose vertexes three elements appear, considered necessary in the processes of linguistic semiosis by a long tradition: the word, the meaning (generally a concept) and the thing referred to (*DeInt.*, 16a 3 – 8).

The dotted line at the bottom of the triangle indicates the indirect nature of the relationship between sound and thing: they are related to each other through a third correlate which in Plato was called the Idea. For Plato, Ideas were abstract entities (conceptual entity – set or class) that were shaped and took Form in concrete individual ways.

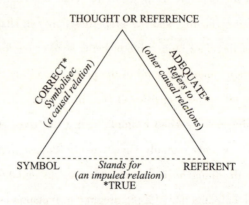

Figure 1   Image of Linguistic Semiosis

The term "universal" came from the translation of Aristotle's *katholou* (*kata holou*) meaning "on the whole" . Although Aristotle rejected certain aspects of Plato's Theory of Forms, but he was also a realist and rejected the position held by the so – called Sophists, which later gave rise to Nominalism, which denies the existence of universals and the existence of transcendent Ideas realized by multiple immanent physical Forms. To Aristotle, all the instances of a name – sign are held together by the exemplification relation, even if this relation is difficult to explain. This discussion reflecting logic, dialectic and rhetoric was, to a great extent, the lines of development for a comprehensive theory on semiosis. Aristotle contributed to define the field in his *Rhetoric*, where he was interested in the proving capacity of arguments and demonstrative reasoning by means of deduction and induction. He explains that deduction starts from probabilities (*eikóton*) or signs (*sémeia*). A sign demonstrate by making the probability more plausible (possible) (*Rhetoric* I, 2, 1357 a 34 ff. cited in Castañares, 2013: 24). To conceive the sign as attached to inferences will be decisive in the approach subsequently adopted both by Hellenistic philosophers (Epicureans and Stoics) and Latin Rhetoricians. Among the preserved papyrus, a treatise by the Epicurean philosopher Philodemus of Gadara, who lived in the 1st century BC, known by its abbreviated title, *De Signis*, is probably the first source of the term *semeióseos* (from which C. S. Peirce would derive *semiosis*). Apart from that, both in this treatise and in the *Poetics* (1456b 20 – 21), Aristotle undertakes an extraordinary work of definition of linguistic terms such as elocution (*lexis*), element (*stoicheîon*), syllable (*syllabé*), conjunction (*sýndesmos*), name (*ónoma*), verb (*rhêma*), article (*árthron*), case (*ptosis*), statement (*logos*), etc.

Returning to the question of imitation and mimesis, when Aristotele writes that a tragedy is an imitation, this meant to the ancient reader that the tragedy was characterized as an image, not a real thing, i. e. the tragedy was seen as something man – made with the sole purpose of creating mental images (perceptions) in the mind of the perceiver, images which the perceiver knows do not represent or answer to real things.

The important thing when discussing imitations is not the imitation as an external thing and its similarities to other external objects but the mental image it triggers, i. e. , the fact that the spectator sees or hears an individual object which he or she knows is not a real thing. This man – made dream produced for those who are awake can be triggered by a number of different kinds of things. Aristotle (*Poetics*, ch. I) distinguishes between kinds of imitations with reference to the medium used, such as words, gestures, shapes, colours, etc. The external imitation object does not necessarily physically resemble the things it represents but rather results in a mental image representing something individual.

Both Plato and Aristotle maintain that music is imitative in character. For example. Aristotle states in *The Politics* that "musical times and tunes provide us with images of states of character". It makes sense to claim within the outline of the theory of imitation sketched here that music is a form of imitation. The sounds we hear are similar to expressions of sadness we have met with before in real life, a representation and expression of sadness. Aristotle writes in *De anima* that "when we form an opinion that something is threatening or frightening, we are immediately affected by it, and the same is true of our opinion that inspires courage; but in imagination we are like spectators looking at something dreadful or encouraging in a picture". And in the *Poetics* he notes that, "[o]bjects which in themselves we view with pain. We delight to contemplate when reproduced with minute fidelity: such as the forms of the most ignoble animals and dead bodies. " This position is inherited by most of the Greek scholars who wrote on aesthetics after Aristotle.

Semiotics after Plato and Aristotle

The Stoic theory of the sign was the foundation of Stoic logic. According to Sextus Empiricus (*Adv. math.* II, 245 cited in Kretzmann, 1967: 364), the sign in Stoic philosophy is an antecedent proposition in a valid hypothetical major premise, which serves to reveal the consequent, so that semiosis is a process of syllogistic induction. From the observable signifier, we infer by mediation of the signified in a process of drawing a logical conclusion about what the sign stands for.

Under the influence of Democritus (ca. 460 – ca. 370), the school of Epicurus (341 – 270) defended a materialist epistemology according to which sensations are impressions made on the soul by images of atoms from the surface of physical objects. The Roman poets Horace and Lucretius (99 – 55) belonged to the Epicurean School, described in a treatise by Philodemus of Gadara to which Peirce made several references. For the Epicurean, the referent of a sign was identified with a sense impression of feeling, rejecting the inferential account of semiosis of the Stoics.

Neoplatonist Christian philosopher St. Augustine (BCE 354 – 430) put forth one of the first theories on sign systems. Augustine defined natural signs as those found in nature and in response to physical and emotional states. St. Augustine distinguished between natural and "conventional" signs, the Last made by humans. He also distinguished what he considered as "sacred" signs, which contained messages from God, and can only be understood by those who has faith. St. Augustine anticipated conceptualism, an intermediate position between realism and nominalism, in his tenet that universal are contained within God's mind, having no external or substantial reality (Coseriu, 1970: 123).

Dissatisfied with the problem of universal signs, medieval scholastics was divided between the realists and the nominalists, who issued an endless debate throughout the Middle – Ages. The scholastic dispute about the nature of the universals concerned the question of the ontological status and the relationship between the signs for general concepts and their objects of reference. Universal was the term used to designate concepts (ideas) of a general nature, empirical objects of the world, experienced as individual entities. The predicates ascribed to them in the form or words were termed "universals" . Thus, whereas the object is particular, the general term designating it is universal. The problem was then the nature of these universals and if they had a reality outside the system of signs. The realists asserted that signs captured universal, God made, Truth (with capitals). Following Plato, they maintained that universals were ideas existing independently of particular objects, *Universalia sunt ante res* (they exist before the things), and that every individual thing participates in the universals of its class. William of Champeaux (1070 – 1120) and Anselm of Canterbury (1033 – 1109) were among the proponents of this so – called extreme realism.

The nominalists, however, argued that only individuals exist in nature, and that truth was a matter of subjective considerations, so that, signs were only illusory versions of the "real" world designed by God and inapprehensible to humans. Thus, for the nominalists, signs only referred to other signs, rather than to actual things. In their view, the universals do not refer to anything and are only names or vocal emissions, so that *universalia sunt post yes* (they alter the things). Roscelin (1050 – 1125) and later William of Ockham (1285 – 1349) were proponents of a nominalist theory of universals.

A moderate realism, also called "conceptualism", was accepted as a synthesis between nominalism and realism by Peter Abelard (1079 – 1142), Albert the Great (1200 – 1280), and Thomas Aquinas (1225 – 1274). In the conceptualist view, the universals are also mind – dependent, but it was maintained that the concepts of the mind were formed by real similarities between things of a common form. In 1474, Louis XI ordered to follow writings by conceptualists such as Aquinas and John Duns Scotus (c. 1266 – 1308) and to ban books by nominalist scholars such as Ockham from lectures at the University of Paris.

The Spanish philosopher Ramon Lull (1232 – 1316) developed a somewhat esoteric theological semiotics in his *Ars Magna* and *Ars Generalis Ultima* (1308). Based on an alphabet of predicates reflecting God's nature, he proposed a logical calculus and *ars inventiva* which he considered to be a key to the interpretation of the universe. Leibniz was also influenced by Lull's ideas in his universal language project (Yates, 1954).

Medieval semiotics

In the late thirteenth and early fourteenth centuries, a theory of signifying modes was also developed by the Dacia School, including Martin of Dacia (Ca. 1270), Boechius of Dacia (Ca. 1270), John of Dacia (ca. 1280), as well as Thomas of Erfurt (ca. 310). They were convinced of an essential iconicity between things of the world and the structure of language. Because of this iconic dependence on the nature of things, all languages, according to the Modists, have an underlying universal structure. In important figure in this respect was Roger Bacon (ca. 1214 – 1292), who declared that "with respect to its *substance*, grammar is one and the same in all languages, although it does vary accidentally" (Gabler, 1987: 23). The universal grammar developed by the Modists was also called *speculative* (*grammatica speculativa et universalis*). This term, derived from Lat. speculum "mirror", expresses the assumption of language being an icon of reality.

The Modists distinguish three dimensions of linguistic semiosis, *res* (thing), *intellectus* (understanding), and *vox* (vocal noise). These modes were associated with these dimensions, the mode of being (*modus essendi*), which provides the ontological foundation of semiosis and the categories of things (their substance, quality, and so on), the mode of understanding and conceptualization (*modus intelligendi*), and the mode of signification (*modus significandi*), which encompasses the semantic functions of the verbal sign, where the vocal signifier is connected with a specific referent in a relation which is arbitrary and language specific (Kretzmann, 1967: 375) By a secondary act of imposition, the word is associated with various modes of signifying which derive from its grammatical form. All grammatical categories or parts of speech are interpreted as having general semantic features which combine with the basic lexical meaning of the word. The semantic relation of these modes is therefore called *consignification* (*ratio consignificandi*). These "consignified" meanings are not arbitrary. They correspond to modes of understanding of the concept and are therefore universal. The modes of signifying are thus a form created by the intellect, which relates the word to the mode of being of the things. The study of these universal categorical dimensions of language forms the core of modist semiotics. Examples of modist views of language as an icon of reality are their interpretations of word classes such as nouns, verbs, or pronouns: "The noun is defined by reference to its 'essential' mode of signifying substances, permanent states or entities. The verb is the part of speech that signifies by the modes of change, becoming, movement of existence. The pronoun signifies substance without reference to any qualities" (Robins 1951: 83).

The Renaissance

During the Renaissance, contributions to semiotics came from Domingo de Soto (1494 – 1560), Pedro de Fonseca (1528 – 1599), and Thomas Campanella (1568 – 1639). In the Enlightenment, British empiricist Thomas Hobbes (1588 – 1679) distinguished between marks and signs in the mental successions of mind conceptions created by the senses and the use of memory. Whereas marks are sign vehicles "for our own use" only, signs serve for the purpose of communicating with others. By means of signs, "what one man finds out may be made known to others" (1655: 2. 2). Marks of "conceptions", according to Hobbes, are names. "A *name* [...] is the voice of a man arbitrary, imposed for a mark to bring into his mind some conception concerning the thing on which it is imposed" (1640: 5. 2). In other words, names given to many things are universal.

John Locke (1632 – 1704) introduced the formal study of signs into philosophy in his *Essay Concerning Human Understanding* (1690: IV. 21.4), where the "doctrine of signs" is defined as $\Sigma \eta\mu\epsilon\iota\omega\tau\iota\kappa\eta$ (1690: IV. 443). Locke proposed this term but he did not use it systematically. The word reappears more frequently in Johann Heinrich Lambert's *Neues Organon* (1764), whose second volume is entitled *Semiotik* (*Semiotics, or the Doctrine of the Designation of Ideas and Things*). Signs, according to Locke, are instruments of knowledge and there are two kinds of them: ideas and words ("articulate sounds"). To him, all ideas come from sensation about external sensible objects, or from reflecti on—internal operations of our minds. So that ideas are signs and words are signs of ideas, that is, signs of signs (or metasigns). Words, according to Locke, make only sense to the person who uses them. They are marks of the ideas in the mind and used to communicate. However, according to Kretzmann, Locke fail to recognize that "words are themselves ideas and the signification of words is a special case of the connection of ideas" (1976: 332, 347). Locke viewed semiotics not merely as a theory but as what Locke called a *doctrine* of signs (1690: 361 – 362), as Sebeok first pointed out (1985: *Foreword* ix), where "doctrine" has a unique sense within the Renaissance mainstream, understanding philosophical knowledge in terms of empirical as well as theological formulations, that is, both scientific and humanistic. Thus, semiotics begins to be contemplated as a perspective concerned with the matrix of all the disciplines.

Against Locke, George Berkeley (1685 – 1753) maintained that words do not always stand for ideas, There are other functions of words, such as "the raising of some passion, the exciting to or deterring from an action, [and] the putting the mind in some particular disposition" (1710: 20; cited in Coseriu, 1972: 58 – 66). It was Saussure who expressed the antithesis to Locke's view of the sign in his simile of the word and idea (signifier and signified) being inseparably connected like the front and the back of a sheet of paper.

Gottfried Wilhelm Leibniz (1646 – 1716) is one of the classics in the history of semiotics. He extended the notion of sign to include not just letters and words but also chemical terminology, astronomical locations, musical notes, arithmetic and algebraic notation, hieroglyphs, Chinese writing and so on. To Leibniz, signs may be arbitrary by themselves, but the principles of their connection to rational discourse are not. There is a relation (*proportio sive relatio*) between the structures of rational discourse and the things of the world which, according to Leibniz, is the foundation of truth. This relation of proportion is, thus, based on diagrammatic iconicity. Indirectly, this implies a triadic model of the sign where it first represents an idea, which stands for a thing/object.

The Enlightenment and the Romantic period

In the context of eighteenth – century hermeneutics and aesthetics, an excursus on the Neapolitan Giambattista Vico (1668 – 1744) and his *New Scince* (1725), a book that inspired James Joyce's novel *Finnegans Wake*. The evolution of signs and humanity are the topics of semiotic relevance in Vico's work where poetry, myth, and metaphor were archaic modes of thought and language. Vico believed in a cyclic conception of history during which mankind has gone through three phases of development called the divine age, the heroic age, and the human age. These phases constitute cycles with a return (or *ricorso*) to earlier stages of development. During the divine age, men "thought everything was a god or was made or done by a god" (Vico, 1725: 922). It was an age of ritual semiosis with "mute religious acts or divine ceremonies" (Vico, 1725: 929). Before developing articulate speech, men communicated by means of divine hieroglyphics (Vico, 1725: 933) or "expressed themselves by means of gestures or physical objects which had natural relations the ideas" (Vico, 1725: 431). Spoken language was developed from onomatopoeia (Vico, 1725: 447 – 48), "a language with natural significations" (Vico, 1725: 431). The dominant mode of communication during the heroic age was by means of visual emblems, coats of arms, ensigns, and other symbols of ownership (Vico, 1725: 484 – 487). Abstract ideas were expressed in the anthropomorphic form of mythical heroes. The third age, the age of men, is the age of reason and of civilization. Signs become arbitrary and abstract, with a decline of poetry and imagination. The ancient mythologies are contemplated as early poetic expressions of human wisdom (Vico, 1725: 352).

The rise of aesthetics in German enlightenment is closely associated with the works Immanuel Kant (1724 – 1804), Gotthold Ephraim Lessing (1729 –

1781), and Moses Mendelssohn (1729 – 1786). The principle of imitation in painting was considered to be the paradigm of this aesthetic iconicity. As to poetry, the aestheticians sought explanations to reconcile the aesthetic ideal of iconicity with the arbitrariness and linearity of the signs used in verbal languages.

The period of romanticism (approximately 1790 and 1830), encompassed works by figures such as Friedrich Wilhelm Schelling (1775 – 1854) and Novalis (Friekdrich von Hardenberg, 1772 – 1801), who continued to hold that human cognition has an iconic nature and that the signs of nature are the words of the universe speaking. Georg Wilhelm Friedrich Hegel (1770 – 1831) defined art as a phenomenon whose essence is neither in the perception of an immediately given signifier, nor in the awareness of the signifier—signified difference which characterizes signs. To Hegel, the semiotic status of art is situated between two semiotic dimensions, the sensuous presence transmuted in semblance of the perceived objective world, and the ideality of pure thought, a form of the "universe".

The tradition of explicit semiotic philosophy was continued by Bernard Bolzano (1781 – 1848), who developed a general "doctrine of signs" (*Zeichenlehre*), which includes a branch of applied studies in Semiotik in his *Theory of Science* (1837). Bolzano defined the sign according to a pragmatic criterion as an object we use with the intention of reviving an idea associated to it in thinking. He distinguished between the meaning (*Bedeutung*) which the sign has in general, and its sense or significance (*Sinn*), which it has in the particular circumstances of its use. He also discussed visual and auditory signs, gestural and verbal signs.

Twenty century semiotics

Edmund Husserl (1859 – 1938) inaugurates twentieth – century semiotics with his phenomenological theory of signs and meaning developed in the paper "On the Logic of Signs (Semiotics)" (1890, published in 1970) and the second volume of his *Philosophical Investigations* (1900 – 1901). Husserl's was an important influence on Prague School structuralism and in Roman Jakobson's theories. Hussel postulated a semiotic threshold that begins above a level of presemiotic intuition of the phenomena (1913: 99). This threshold lies between the spheres of immediate perception and symbolic conception (*Vorstellung*). At the level of perception, an object is given in it immediate appearance. Although perceptual cognition is based on sense impressions, it occurs without the mediation of signs. At this level, the essence of things (*eidos*) can be grasped only by phenomenological intuition (*Wesensschau*). Above the semiotic threshold, by contrast a phenomenon is no longer perceived "in itself". but "with the awareness (*Bewußtsen*) that it represents something else or indicates it signitively" (ibid.). The distinction between the semiotic and the nonsemiotic world is thus a distinction between the immediate awareness of the phenomena and the awareness of the "otherness" of the perceived object, which implies the cognition of a difference between the signifier and the signified.

In the twentieth-century, authors to be included in the history of semiotics are Alfred North Whitehead (1861 – 1947), Bertrand Russell (1672 – 1970), Ludwig Wittgenstein (1889 – 1951) and Charles Sanders Peirce (1839 – 1914), Ferdinand de Saussure (1857 – 1913), and Thomas Albert Sebeok (1920 – 2001), among others who will be described in the following lines.

Swiss linguist Ferdinand de Saussure is considered to be the founder of linguistics and semiology. In 1906, Saussure took the place of Joseph Wertheimer at the University of Geneva and taught three courses in general linguistics, in 1906 – 1907, 1908 – 1909, and 1910 – 1911. The first edition of his notes, under the title, *Complete Course in General Linguistics*, was published in Geneva in July 1915 by Charles Bally, Albert Sechehaye, and it was translated from the French by Wade Baskin for the New York Philosophical Library in 1959. In his notes, Saussure postulated the existence of a general science of signs or semiology, of which linguistics would form part. In the introduction to his book, Saussure looks at the history of the study of signs from its origins in Greek poetics. Saussure explains that "comparative philology" is born only in the late 18th –

century when Anglo – Welsh philologist and orientalist, established in West Bengal, Sir William Jones (1746 – 1794) who postulated the existence of a relationship among Indo – European languages. But it was not until the 19th – century, when Franz the German Sanskrit scholar Franz Bopp (1791 – 1867) compared Sanskrit to German, as well as Greek and Latin, establishing similarities among these languages belonging to the Indo – European family.

Under Structuralist semiology, a text isan assemblage of signs (such as words, images, sounds and/or gestures), intended to be communicated (message), constructed by the sender and interpreted by the receiver with reference to the conventions associated with a given culture (code) in a particular medium of communication (channel). All these elements form what Roman Jacobson termed the "context" of communication (see following chapter). However, texts can also refer to messages which have been recorded in some way (for example, in writing, audio – and video – recording) so that it is physically independent of its sender or receiver.

Saussure also distinguished between "language", which refers to a cultural system of rules and conventions which is independent of the individual use of signs, and "speech", which he used to refer to individual language use (specific to a person). Saussure placed more importance on the overall general structure failing to account for particular cases dependent on context change (for example, the use of a different channel, such as video, where signs are not just textual but also moving images). In disagreement with Saussure, the Russian linguist Valentin Voloshinov (1895 – 1936) proposed a reversal of the Saussurean priority, language over speech, claiming that such ideal level of organizational communication cannot exist. He argued that meaning is not just in the relationship of a sign to other signs within the system (syntagmatic axis), as Saussure had proposed, but rather in its changing (paradigmatic axis) social context and use, and idea also stressed by the German philosopher of language Ludwig Wittgenstein (1889 – 1951).

Saussure believed that all signs (images, gestures, as well as verbal language) shared discursive properties, that is, had a textual/narrative structure. When commenting on different signs and media, semiologists use a vocabulary more appropriate to the study of written texts and literature. In this sense, images, whether fixed or in movement, as in TV or cinema, can be read and interpreted. For example, one of first books to push the boundaries of television studies published in 1978 by John Fiske and John Hartley, spoke of the grammar of TV documentaries and used the analogy with language to speak about images.

Despite Saussure's attempt to clarify how words might "name" objects surrounds, as Wittgenstein puts it, the workings of language with a haze that makes clear vision impossible (Wittgenstein, 1958: 4). Saussure tried to get around this problem by saying that the linguistic sign does not unite a thing and a name, but a concept and a sound image (Saussure, 1971: 98). In the case of written language, the sign consists of the printed form of a word and a concept. In the case of an image, the sign consist of a set of shapes, colors and shades, and a concept.

For Saussure and other Structuralists, sign systems were constituted emphasizing differences and oppositions to other elements within the system. Saussure used an analogy with the game of chess, noting that the value of each piece depends on its position on the chessboard (Saussure, 1974: 88). He saw both the signifier and the signified as non – material psychological forms; the language itself is "a form, not a substance" (Saussure, 1974: 113, 122) Saussure uses several examples to reinforce his point. In the chess analogy, he notes that "if pieces made of ivory are substituted for pieces made of wood, the change makes no difference to the system" (Saussure, 1974: 22). He admits that "linguistic signs are, so to speak, tangible: writing can fix them in conventional images" (Saussure, 1974: 15). However, referring to written signs, he comments that "the actual mode of inscription is irrelevant, because it does not affect the system... Whether I write in black or white, in incised characters or in relief, with a pen or a chisel – none of that is of any importance for the meaning" (Saussure, 1974: 120). Thus, language for Saussure is a system of functional differences and oppositions: "In a language, as in every other semiological system, what distinguishes a sign is what constitutes it" (Saussure, 1974: 121). Meaning arises from differences between signifiers. These differences are of two kinds: syntagmatic (concerning positioning) and paradigmatic (concerning substitution). *Synchronic* means analytic and *diachronic* means historical, so a synchronic study of a text looks at the relationships that exist among its elements, and a diachronic study looks at the way the narrative evolves. These two dimensions are represented as two axes, where the horizontal is the syntagmatic and the paradigmatic is the vertical. A syntagm is a chain, and in syntagmatic analysis, a text is examined as a sequence of events that forms some kind of narrative. It comprises a set of arbitrary sign units that conform a structure. For example, a group of syllables forms a word, and a string of words a sentence, where each word has a function. Sign units enter into a paradigmatic relation when you can substitute one for another. In conducting a synchronic analysis of a text, one looks for the pattern of paired oppositions buried in the text (the paradigmatic structure), whereas in doing diachronic analysis, one focuses on the chain of events (the syntagmatic structure) that forms the narrative (Saussure, 1974: 119). The paradigmatic analysis of a text involves a search for a hidden pattern of oppositions that are buried in it and that generate meaning. The paradigmatic form of structural analysis seeks to describe the pattern (usually based upon an a priori binary principle of opposition). Saussure makes a distinction between static synchronic and evolutionary diachronic semiology, explaining that:

> All sciences would prof it by indicating more precisely the coordinates along which their subject matter is aligned. Everywhere distinctions should be made... between (1) *the axis of simultaneity*... which stands for the relations of coexisting things and from which the intervention of time is excluded; and (2) *the axis of successions* [···] on which only one thing can be considered at a time but upon which are located all the things on the first axis together with their changes (Saussure, 1974: 79 – 80) .

To explain the differences between these two perspectives, Saussure suggests that the reader imagine a plant. If one makes a longitudinal cut in the stem of a plant, one sees the fibers that make up the plant, but if one makes a cross – sectional cut, one can see the plant's fibers in relationship to each another.

Saussaure focused on speech, and made a distinction between *langue* (language) and *parole* (speech). *Langue* refers to the system of rules and conventions which is independent of individual use; *parole* refers to its use in particular instances. Applying the notion to semiotic systems in general rather than simply to language, the distinction is one between *code* and *message*. Seeking the general underlying structures and rules of signification, Saussure focused on the synchronic (in a particular space – time) study of *langue*, rather than specific uses (*parole*) or its diachronic evolution. A functional approach was generally adopted by structural theorists, who failed to account for changes in language structure. Thus, structuralist analysis focused on the structural relations which are functional in the signifying system at a particular moment in history, and which is built upon sociocultural conventions. This is more or less clear in the case of the linguistic signs, which were the object of Saussure's interest, but it did not explain the particularities of other visual signs, such as those used in the medium of photography, for instance.

One of the most important problem in Saussure's conception, which gave way to postmodern argumentations was the fact that if one accepts the arbitrariness of the relationship between signifier and signified then it might be argued that the signified is determined by the signifier rather than vice versa. Subsequent theorists have emphasized the temporary nature of the bond between signifier and signified, stressing that the "fixing" of "the chain of signifiers" is socially situated. In the late 1920s, Valentin Volosinov (1884/5 – 1936) and Mikhail Bakhtin (1895 – 1975) criticized Saussure's synchronic approach and his emphasis on internal relations within the system of language, arguing that "The sign is part of organized social intercourse and cannot exist, as such, outside it, reverting to a mere physical artifact" (Voloshinov, 1973, 21). He added that "a synchronic system may be said to exist only from the point of view of the subjective consciousness of an individual speaker belonging to some particular language group at some particular moment of historical time" (Voloshinov, 1973, 66). Voloshinov described Saussure's ideas as "the most striking expression" of "abstract objectivism" (Voloshinov, 1973: 58), and insisted that "a sign is a phenomenon of the external world" and that "signs... are particular, material things" with "some kind of material embodiment, whether in sound, physical mass, colour, movements of the body, or the like" (Voloshinov, 1973: 28), so that all signs have "concrete material reality" (Voloshinov, 1973: 65) so that the physical properties of the sign matter. Other Marxist scholars, like the members of the Prague School of Linguists, also argued that the meaning of signs does not arise from their inter – relationships within the language system but from their use in particular social contexts, as part of their social use within a "code" (see below), where signs acquire a kind of "history" familiar to the users within that culture (see denotation and connotation below).

Roughly around the same time as Saussure presented his theory of the linguistic sign, American logician Charles Sanders Peirce (1832 – 1914) defended a broader definition of signs that included (1) artificial or formal languages (mathematical) and natural languages (symbols), that are arbitrary (decided upon by a given community; for instance, French, English or Chinese; other examples include morse code, traffic lights, national flags and so on; Peirce, 1931 – 58: 2. 249; 2. 292; 2. 297; 2. 299) (2)❶ signs that refer to objects by means of semblances and similarities of some perceptual qualities (i. e. a portrait, a scale – model, photographs, maps, onomatopoeic sounds, sound effects in radio/video soundtracks, imitative gestures and so on; Peirce called them "icons"; Peirce 1931 –58: 2. 247; 2. 276; 2. 279; 3. 362), and (3) signs mode in which the signifier is *not* arbitrary but is connected in some way (physically or causally) to

---

❶   The designation CP abbreviates *The Collected Papers of Charles Sanders Peirce*, Vols. I – VI ed. Charles Hartshorne and Paul Weiss. Cambridge, MA: Harvard University Press, 1931—1935; Vols. VII – VIII ed. Arthur W. Burks Cambridge, MA: Harvard University Press, 1958. The abbreviation followed by volume and paragraph numbers with a period between follows the standard CP reference form.

the signified—this link can be observed or inferred (i. e. chemical reactions, smoke, thunder, footprints, medical symptoms such as fever, measuring instruments such as a thermometer, signals like a phone ringing, pointers like a finger or a signpost, indexical terms such as here/there, today/tomorrow, you/I, and so on) which Peirce called these "indexes" (Peirce, 1931 – 58: 2. 281; 2. 285; 2. 231; 2. 310; 4. 447).

Peirce sought formal philosophical ways to articulate thought's processes, including both natural languages, those used in the humanities, and the formal mathematical languages used in science. Thus, starting from the oldest Western sources found mainly in Plato, Aristotle and Locke, Peirce developed a description of sign relations and of their interpretation by means of analogic thought as well as three different modes of mental inference: abduction, deduction and induction. Each type of sign shows different degrees of conventionality, with symbols being more arbitrary and indexes and icons more constrained by their referents or signifieds (Peirce, 1931 – 58: 2. 306) Iconic and indexical signs are more likely to be seen as "natural" than symbolic signs when making the connection between signifier and signified has become habitual. Indexicality is based on an act of judgement or inference, whereas iconicity is closer to "direct perception".

Peirce noted that different material media can mediate a conjunction of signs. For example, a photography may be both iconic and indexical (Peirce, 1931 – 58: 2. 281; 4. 447; 5. 554) as it is produced by the effect of light on a chemical emulsion. Once edited, photographic images may resemble what they depict, and thus be icons. Iconicity and indexicality are dependent on the properties of medium, and also on the genre conventions used. For example, John Lyons has argued that a word might be iconic in a phonic medium (i. e. onomatopoeic words such as zig – zag or cuckoo) and not be so in the graphic written medium which does not capture the sound effect (Lyons, 1977: 103, 105). The genre is also important because documentary film, for instance, can increase the indexical quality of representation in order to warrant the status of the material as proof or evidence.

Thus, whether a sign is symbolic, iconic or indexical depends on the way in which the sign is used, and on the material modalities of its display (Peirce, 1931 – 58. 2: 304). In advertising, for instance images can take connotative meanings that make, for instance, a car, become a symbol of wealth and social status. Peirce's theory of signs remained undiscovered for many years and is generally attributed to Roman Jakobson. The standard edition of Peirce's works is his *Collected Papers* (CP 1931 – 58).

Unlike Saussure, who contemplated representation as merely linguistic, composed of signified (the physical object) and signifier (the sign used to refer to the object), for Peirce this relation was triadic, involving not just the object and the sign, but also what he termed "interpretant". He explained that "a sign... is something which stands to somebody for something in some respect or capacity" (Peirce, 1931 – 58: 2. 228) . Semiosis is, then, the "action, or influence, which is, or involves, a cooperation of three elements, the sign, its object, and its interpretant (not a personal intelligence but another kind of sign – in – process, so to say) this tri – relative influence not being in any way resolvable into actions between pairs" (Peirce Collected Papers, 1907; reprinted in "Pragmatism" 398 – 433). For Peirce, all thought is in signs and their interpretation (Peirce, 1931 – 58, 1. 538), closely related to the ways logic thinking works (Peirce, 1931 – 58, 2. 227). In other words, only the perception of things around us can trigger mental processes. The sign (he also calls it "representamen" because in its broadest sense it "represents") functions as a mediator between the world of objects and the mind.

As Sebeok noted, unlike Saussure's glottocentric approach, Peirce's understanding incorporated an understanding of culture as constituted by multiple types of signs, including semblances, diagrams, metaphors, symptoms, signals, designations, symbols, texts, even mental concepts and ideas.

The chronology of semiotic inquiry so far, viewed panoramically, exhibits an oscillation between two seemingly antithetical tendencies: in the major tradition (which I am tempted to christen a Catholic heritage), semiosis takes its place as a normal occurrence of nature, of which, to be sure, language—that paramount known mode of terrestrial communication which is Lamarckian in style, that is, embodies a learning process that becomes part of the evolutionary legacy of the ensuing generations—forms an important if relatively recent component [⋯] The minor trend, which is parochially glottocentric, asserts, sometimes with sophistication but at other times with embarrassing naivete, that linguistics serves as the model for the rest of semiotics—Saussure's *le patron générale*—because of the allegedly arbitrary and conventional character of the verbal sign (Sebeok, 1977: 181).

Thus, linguistic signs may well be "the ideological phenomenon par excellence", as Voloinov said (1973: 13); but the action of signs, which provides the general subject matter of semiotic inquiry, extends well beyond what we call language.

Peirce explained that a sign is something, A, which brings something, B, its *interpretant* sign, determined or created by it, into the same sort of correspondence (or a lower implied sort) with something, C, its *object*, as that in which itself stands to C. (Peirce, 1896 CP 1. 417 – 520). The sign as mediator exists no as a "thing" but as a potential "relation" to the other elements. In other words, the sign of an object (which can be physical but also a memory, or even something imaginary/fictional) leads to one or more interpretants, which in turn, as signs, lead to further interpretants (they are kind of meaningful ramifications formed into a kind of concept/idea or emotional response). An important factor is that the sign arises in the "experience" of the object (whether physical/perceptual or already mental/remembered).

Peircean semiotics includes the possibility of contemplating not just verbal languages and gestures as signs, but also other cultural elements such as visual art, clothing patterns, as well as any other human practices in whatever medium (not just textual). However, Peirce's sign categories are not mutually exclusive. A sign could very well be all three at the same time. For example, TV uses all three at the same time, when the figure of the newsreader (iconic) is telling the news, the words he/she uses are symbolic, but the effect of the film that accompanies the information is both iconic and indexical.

Peirce's emphasis on pragmatism also moved away from the structuralist classification of sign systems and how meanings are made (semantics) in order to explore communication as action, that is, how it construct reality (pragmatism). He helped to show that information or meaning is not "contained" in the world, in books or objects. Meaning is not "transmitted" to us—we continually and actively create meaning.

Peirce's semiotics is based upon his system of categories. While Aristotle had postulated ten, and Kant twelve, ontological categories, Peirce developed a phenomenology based on only three universal categories called *firstness*, *secondness*, and *thirdness*. "*Firstness* is the mode of being of that which is such as it 15, positively and without reference to anything else. " (CP 8. 328) It is the category of the unreflected feeling, potentiality, freedom, immediacy, and undifferentiated quality (CP 1. 30 2 – 303, 1. 328, 1. 531). *Secondness* involves the relation of a first to a second (CP 1. 356 – 59) and is used for comparison, facts, action, and experience in time and space: *Thirdness* brings a second in relation to a third (CP 1. 337) and it is the category of mediation and semiosis, of habit, memory, continuity, synthesis, communication and representation. Signs are phenomena of thirdness and stand, as explain before, in a triadic relation between a first sign (representamen) and second (its object) and the third determined by them (interpretant) (CP 2. 274).

A sign, or *representamen*, is something which stands to somebody for something in some respect or capacity. It addresses somebody, that is creates in the mind of that person an equivalent sign, or perhaps a more developed sign. That sign which it creates I call the *interpretant* of the first sign. The sign stands for something, its object stands for that object, not in all respects, but in reference to a sort of idea (CP 2. 228).

As mentioned, Peirce classifiesd signs with respect to the relation between the representamen and object (CP 2. 275) so that icons are in firstness indexes in secondness, and symbols in thirdness. Thus, "a Symbol is a sign which refers to the object that it denotes by virtue of a law, usually an association of general ideas" (CP 2. 449). From the point of view of its object relation, the textual sign is poly – functional: it is a symbol insofar as it consists of arbitrary signs, but it is also indexical when its primary function is conative (appellative), as in commands, instructions and questions. The textual reference to persons, objects and events in a spatiotemporal context are all forms of indexicality. Textual iconicity takes form of images, diagrams, and metaphors. Visual poetry and onomatopoeic poems are examples of texts functioning as images.

Another important figure in 20th – century semiotics is Charles William Morris (1901 – 1979) who envisioned semiotics "on a biological basis and specif ically within the framework of the science of behavior" (1946: 80). Morris intended to contribute to the project of a "Unified Science", "both a science among the sciences and an instrument of the sciences" (Morris 1938: 2). Morris described semiosis as a process of semiotic mediation: "A sign is used with respect to some goal if it is produced by an interpreter as a means of attaining that goal; a sign that is used is thus a means – object" (1946: 368). Morris indicated that the same internal and formal relations of signs to each other in formal structures (syntax) found in languages were then applied to the level of meaning (semantics) in order to explore relations between signs and the things they refer to, and finally, relations of signs to their impacts by those who use them in specific social situations (pragmatics). Thus, semiotic embraced semantics as well as other traditional branches of linguistics: *semantics*, the relationship of signs to what they stand for; *syntactics* (or *syntax*), the formal or structural relations between signs; and *pragmatics*, the relation of signs to interpreters (Morris, 1938, 6 – 7).

Like Peirce, the Danish linguist Louis Hjelmslev (1899 – 1965) believed that the suppression of the specific materiality of the sign was also a problem in Saussure and structuralist linguistics. He noted that both expression and content have substance and form, and that the same expression in different forms means different things. The material in itself gives the contents different meaning. Hjelmslev renamed signifier and signified as "expression" and "content" planes, taking into consideration both form (of content and expression) and substance (of content and expression). In this way, the Danish scholar reacted against Saussure's emphasis on oral and written discourse, considering that the material substance of signs can be, for example, hand movements and gestures in sign language for the mute – deaf. The content substance is important, but one needs to analyze it from the point of view of form since in order to establish the basis for *shared* conceptions, ideas must be embodied in a publicly accessible objective structure (not just in the mind). The idea must be correlated with some physical element within experience that is taken to serve as ground for the relation in which the idea expressly consists. That correlation is what constitutes a *code* in its difference from an idea. A code thus channels and directs relations among objects in a publicly accessible way, explains John Deely (1990). Ideologies and values prevalent in a given culture are incorporated into the codes used for communication in that culture, so that "to see cultural life as a web of codes and as a continuous reference from code to code is to restore to the human animal its true nature" (Eco, 1977: 52).

This cultural approach to semiotics became particularly strong in the late 1960s, partly as a result of the work of Roland Barthes (1915 – 1980), particularly of his collection of essays, entitled *Mythologies*. Barthes's work challenged some of the ideas developed by the French anthropologist Claude Lévi – Strauss suggested that a syntagmatic analysis of a text reveals the text's manifest meaning and that a paradigmatic analysis reveals the text's latent meaning. The manifest structure of a text consists of what happens in it, whereas the latent structure consists of what the text is about. Or, to put it another way, when we use a paradigmatic approach, we are not so much concerned with what characters *do* as with what they *mean*. Lévi – Strauss' (1967) study on kinship and ancient communities (1967) reveled an underlying structure of minimal units or "mythemes" expressed in short sentences that describe important relationships in the human groups in which they functioned. These myths, explained Lévi – Strauss, provide coded cultural messages.

On the other hand, for Barthes, the term language should be extended to include written and spoken words, sounds, music, images, or gestures (Barthes, 1978: 9). Like Saussure, Barthes used the termed "semiology" for "any system of signs, whatever their substance and limits; images, gestures, musical sounds, objects, and the complex associations of all of these, which form the content of ritual, convention or public entertainment: these constitute, if not languages, at least systems of signification" (Barthes, 1967: 9). The signifier and signified are separate in theory but work together in a process of connecting some communicative representation with a concept or meaning. A word, sound, or image (signifier) operates simultaneously in association with its conceptual (signified) referent. The association of the signifier and the signified produce the sign through this theoretical correlation which is called *signification* or *semiosis* (Barthes, 1972: 113; Barthes, 1978: 48).

Barthes contributed to extend the work of Russian (later exiled in the United States) semiotician Roman Jakobson (1896 – 1982) who put forward the pivotal notion of "motivated signs", which he defined as the tendency to make signs represent the world through simulation. Barthes explained how the construction of meaning takes place by introducing the idea of different orders/levels of signification. The first order of signification is that of denotation, this is the sign consisting of signifier and signified. In the case of an iconic sign, the photography of an object refers to that object. Connotation is the second order of signification, which uses the denotative sign as its signifier and attaches to it additional signifieds by means of human intervention (for example, introducing lighting, camera angle, and so on). Thus, in "The Rhetoric of the Image" (1977), Barthes argues that in photography the denoted (first – order) meaning is conveyed by means of mechanical processes of reproduction. One example is the use of "Bauhaus 93" font to refer to a classic movie, instead of a modernist theme that the font may suggest: Alice in Wonderland.

The use of certain fonts trigger certain values (connotations) that are deeply rooted in each culture. However, in reality it is difficult to separate the two levels, and Fiske noted that it was often easy to read connotative values in denotative facts (1982). Denotation and connotation combines into the third order of signification, which Barthes calls "myth".

Connotation and denotation are often described in terms of levels of representation or levels of meaning. Roland Barthes adopted from Louis Hjelmslev the notion that there are different orders of signification (Barthes, 1957; Hjelmslev, 1961: 114). The first order of signification is that of denotation: at this level there is a sign consisting of a signifier and a signified. Connotation is a second – order of signification which uses the denotative sign (signifier and signified) as its signifier and attaches to it an additional signified. In this framework, connotation is a sign which derives from the signifier of a denotative sign (so denotation leads to a chain of connotations). This tends to suggest that denotation is an underlying and primary meaning—a notion which many other commentators have challenged. Barthes himself later gave priority to connotation and noted that it was no longer easy to separate the signifier from the signified, the ideological from the literal. In a departure from Hjelmslev's model Barthes argues that the orders of signification called denotation and connotation combine to produce ideology or "myth" (third order signification).

Barthes advanced his interpretation of Saussure's denotative and connotative structures to suggest myth as another level of signification where the "semiological system is a system of values" (1972: 131). Myth builds upon the same process that composes the first and second order of signification. Barthes theorizes that myth carries an order of cultural signification where semiotic code is perceived as fact (1972: 131), therefore assuming a degree of power and authority. There is an already assumed connotative meaning of the sign that seems natural from a particular context of cultural consumption. Thus, myth maintains an inf luential power through a quality of appearing self – evident. Myth subsumes the second order of signification to construct a "global sign" within a system that Barthes calls *metalanguage*, because it is a second language, *in which* one speaks about the f irst" (1972: 115). That recognition begins with what Barthes called "ideological abuse" (1972: 11) which indicates his own ideological dispute with the assumptions embedded in the form the way of communication refers to its content.

Barthes builds his own theory on Hjelmslev's, who offers a method of applied analysis that demonstrates how signification occurs on two distinct levels (Barthes, 1978, 49). This model states "there is a relation (R) between the plane of expression (E) and the plane of content (C)" (Barthes, 1978, 49). The *denotative* first order of signification can thus be represented as (E R C); the correlation of the signifier or expression (E) in relation (R) to the signified or content (C). The problematic ambiguity of the relationship between signifier and signified is no addressed because (R) takes up the context or culture of the expression (E) as the signifier of meaning or content (C). At the *connotative* or second order of signification, the signifier or expression (E2) is constituted by the sum of E R C from the first order of signification (Barthes, 1978, 89 – 90).

In his preface to the 1957 edition of *Mythologies*, Roland Barthes explains the origins of his collection of essays as an attempt to reflect on current events as "some myths of French daily life" (1972: 11). The project of myth analysis lies in articulating the relationship between all aspects of a sign system that constructs meaning around cultural assumptions embedded in the form. To Barthes, myth is a third order of signification, a form that provides understanding derived from, but beyond denotation and connotation. The veracity of meaning is embodied in the framework of communication. For example, "pictures, to be sure, are more imperative than writing, they impose meaning at one stroke, without analysing or diluting it" (Barthes, 1972: 110). For Barthes myths were the dominant ideologies of our time. "Myth has in fact double functions: it points out and it notifies, it makes us understand something and it imposes it on us... It transforms history into nature" writes Barthes in *Mythologies* (1957). Myths can be seen as extended metaphors, made up of signs and codes. Like metaphors (Lakoff and Johnson, *Metaphors we live by*, 1980), myths help us to make sense of our experience within a culture. For Barthes, myths serve the ideological function of naturalization, making dominant historical and cultural values; attitudes and beliefs seem entirely natural, normal or commonsense. Barthes exemplifies this process with the example of a photograph of a black soldier wearing a French uniform in the cover of French magazine *Paris Match*. The soldier seems to be looking up toward the French flag (denotation), but the second order signification (*connotation*) arises from the cultural experience where the soldier (iconic sign) becomes a signifier (symbol) of the greatness of the nation, exemplified by his submissive gaze to the flag. Furthermore, the choice of a "black" soldier seems to emphasize the inclusive character of the nation, including citizens from what once were the nation's colonies.

Third – order signification is a matter of the cultural meanings of signs. These cultural meanings derive not from the sign itself, but from the way that society uses and values the signifier and the signified. Thus, Barthes is concerned here with the *ideological* import of the photograph. He sees myths as organising the cultural meanings we attach to signs, and their main function is to legitimise bourgeo is ideology.

In Britain, the adoption of semiotics was influenced by the prominence of the Centre for Contemporary Cultural Studies at the University of Birmingham under the direction of the neo – Marxist sociologist Stuart Hall, and John Fiske. Fiske explained " 'reality' is always encoded, or rather the only way we can perceive and make sense of reality is by the codes of our culture. There may be an objective, empiricist reality out there, but there is no universal, objective way of perceiving and making sense of it. What passes for reality in any culture is the product of the culture's codes, so 'reality' is always already encoded, it is never 'raw' " (Fiske, 1987: 4 – 5) . British linguist, David Crystal (1987) has also claimed that cultural conventions are involved even if a sign is iconic and would seem closer to reality than other signs. Cultural convention is the social dimension of signs; the means that enable their sharing. Hall makes the case that the relationship of denotation to connotation is useful only as an analytical distinction (1980: 132 – 3). Denotation is not necessarily a literal meaning that can be understood apart from the changeable interpretive meanings associated with connotation. The denotative sign can appear to be universally understood as having a natural meaning. Thus, "we could say that its ideological value is strongly fixed", while connotation is understood through the ideology of its "situational" cultural context (Hall, 1980: 133). The two terms are "useful analytical tools for distinguishing... the different levels at which ideologies and discourses intersect" (Hall, 1980, 133).

Furthermore, because codes are located within specific cultures, it is not surprising that they express and support the social organization of those cultures. From this point of view there is no such thing as meaning which is independent of the ideological and political positions within which language is used, pointing to the way power relationships and hegemonic and power positions are maintained. Thus, French sociologist and anthropologist Pierre Bourdieu (1930 – 2002) considered that every linguistic exchange has the potential to be an act of power. In *Language & Symbolic Power* (1991), he highlighted that the close correspondence between social structures and mental structures, which fulfilled a political function of domination. Placing emphasis on the politics of signification, Western Marxist scholars have attempted to give voice to underprivileged groups (women, blacks, workers and so on; se for instance, Terry Eagleton, 1983).

Much advance in semiotics came from the work of the Society for the Study of Poetic Language (OPOYAZ) founded in 1916 in St. Petersburg (then Petrograd) by Boris Eichenbaum, Viktor Shklovsky and Yury Tynyanov. Later it became associated to the Moscow Linguistic Circle founded in 1914 by Roman Jakobson. Vladimir Propp. These scholars approach the study literature from a scientific and factual point of view, and linguistics was a fundamental aspect. The group studied the formal structures that determine the content of literature (form and content together) in what came to be known as Formalism. "Defamiliarization" is one of the crucial ways in which literary language distinguishes itself from ordinary, communicative language, and is a feature of how art in general works, namely by presenting the world in a strange and new way that allows us to see things differently. The leaders of the movement suffered political persecution beginning in the 1920s, when Joseph Stalin came to power, which largely put an end to their inquiries. But their ideas continued to influence subsequent thinkers, partly due to Tzvetan Todorov's translations of their works in the 1960s and 1970s, including Todorov himself, Roland Barthes and Gerald Genette (see the following chapter).

Roman Jakobson (1896 – 1982) left Moscow for Prague in 1920, a year of political conflict in Russia, Jakobson relocated to Prague to continue his doctoral studies. He immersed himself both into the academic and cultural life of the city, and established close relationships with a number of Czech poets and literary figures. A few years later, Jakobson received his Ph. D. and became a university professor. In 1926, he became one of the founders of the "Prague School" of linguistic theory. The group was dissolved in 1939 when the onset of World War II caused the relocation in the United States of the Jewish Russian émigrés Roman Jakobson Nikolai Trubetzkoy, and René Wellek.

The Prague Linguistic Circle was established by Vilem Mathesius, with Bohuslav Havranek, Josef Hrabak, Jan Mukafovsky, Bohumil Trnka, Jan Vachek and Felix Vodicka. The Russian émigrés Jakobson Trubetzkoy, and Tynianov also joined the group. This fusion brought together the tradition of Opojaz Russian formalism with the Kazan school of Polish linguistics (which focused mainly on phonology) as well as influences from the Swiss Saussurean tradition and German philosophy. From Saussure, they took the differentiation of the language – system from the speech act or speech event. From the tradition of Russian formalism they got the idea that the function of normalizing speech is not the only function of language. From the Polish tradition they took the study of phonology as paradigm for linguistic study in general.

The methodological backbone of Prague structuralism followed two aspects. Firstly, that language and its homological equivalents cannot be explained through reference to extralinguisric factors. Secondly, each research procedure involves: a) separating out of the speech order a class of phenomena with a common dominating function; b) the analysis of other relations with other functions which modify this class; and c) the discovery and description of the language which makes the given phenomena possible. The first rule expresses the methodological principle of immanence, while the second links inductionism to fuctionalism. Although the Saussurean legacy of the Prague Circle is obvious, as mentioned in the previous chapter, it is paradoxical that the concept of structure, which had earlier been absent, appeared in their writing. It was the Circle which produced probably the first systematic questioning of the philosophical grounds of Geneva linguistics. As a result of it, most of the concepts, distinctions and claims of Saussure were rejected or modified. Because of its consequences for aesthetics, one should first of all mention the fact that the Prague Circle were opposed to the unconditional separation of language and speech. This objection took different forms—ranging from the moderate to the extreme. Jakobson gradually inclined towards a belief that even within the dominating social dimension language maintains a trace of its individual dimension, and that speech, with all its individual character, has a social aspect. Finally, there was questioning and rejects of the grounds of Saussure's Leibnizian synchronic determinism. The idea that a pre – existing static language fixes all possible meanings until its displacement by another structure of the same kind was incomprehensible to Jakobson. This gave birth to the idea of a dynamic rather than static, and teleological rather than deterministic, semiotic system, an idea particularly developed in Jan Mukafovsky's conception of semiotics (see the following chapter).

In his way to North – America, Jakobson escaped via Denmark, where he became associated with the Copenhagen linguistic circle, and with Louis Hjelmslev in particular. Hjelmslev's research was concern with the problematic distinction between form and content. He acknowledged that "there can be no content without an expression, or expressionless content; neither can there be an expression without a content, or content – less expression" (Hjelmslev, 1961: 49) and put forth a framework which facilitated analytical distinctions by referring to "planes" of expression and content, that the duality signifier/signified. He indicated that both planes of expression and content have substance and form. The substance of expression included the physical materials of the medium (i. e. printed words, images, photographs, recorded voice or film), form of expression (language, syntax, style...) substance of content (subject matter, genre) and form of content (semantic and narrative structure). Thus, Hjelmslev's framework broadens the notion of what constitutes a sign, taking into consideration its materiality.

As the war advanced west, Jakobson was smuggled into Norway in a coffin with his wife. When Swedish colleagues feared for a possible German occupation, he managed to leave on a private yacht, together with Ernst Cassirer (the former rector of Hamburg University) to New York City to become part of the wider community of intellectual émigrés. In 1949 Jakobson moved to Harvard University, where he remained until retirement. In his last decade he maintained an office at the Massachusetts Institute of Technology, where he was an honorary Professor Emeritus.

Jakobson and Trubetzkoy developed techniques for the analysis of sound systems in languages, inaugurating the discipline of phonology. Then Jakobson went on to apply the same techniques of analysis to syntax and morphology, and controversially proposed that they be extended to semantics (the study of meaning in language). ❷ Drawing on insights from Charles Sanders Peirce as well as from communication theory he proposed methods for the investigation of poetry, mu-

---

❷   Jakobson's framework included studies in phonology (sounds in language), morphology (the form of linguistic signs), syntax (formal properties of signs), semantics (study of relationships between signs and what they represent; in other words, meaning) and pragmatic (concerned with the relations between signs and their users).

sic, the visual arts, and cinema. Jakobson envisioned communication as a process governed by various levels:

(1) An information source (sender) / transmitter or encoder (machine), which produces a message and encodes the message into signs (or signals in the case of a transmitte).

(2) A channel or medium to which signs/signals are adapted for transmission.

(3) A receiver/decoder which "decodes" (reconstructs) the message from the signs/signals.

Jakobson also distinguished six communication functions, each associated with a dimension or factor of the communication process:

(1) referential (contextual information)

(2) aesthetic/poetic (auto – reflection)

(3) emotive (self – expression)

(4) conative (vocative or imperative addressing of receiver)

(5) phatic (checking channel working)

(6) metalingual (checking code working)

One of the six functions is always the dominant function in a text and usually related to the type of text. In poetry, the dominant function is the poetic function: the focus is on the message itself. The true hallmark of poetry and literariness is, according to Jakobson, the fact that it successfully combines and integrates form and function (Sebeok, 1960: 350 – 377). Thus, the objective elements in any act of communication are constituted by

· The message, formed in turn by signs of any kind.

· The code used to encrypt the message.

· The context, constituted in turn by the space in which communication of message and the time when this occurs is performed.

· The channel through which the message is transmitted.

Through his decisive influence on Claude Lévi – Strauss and Roland Barthes, among others, Jakobson became a pivotal figure in the adaptation of structural analysis to disciplines beyond linguistics, including literary theory.

Jakobson's compatriot René Wellek taught first at the University of Iowa and then at Yale University. With Austin Warren, Wellek published a landmark volume entitled *Theory of Literature*, one of the first works to systematize literary theory. Beginning in the 1960s, Wellek defended the New Critics (Chicago School) against the condemnation of their work in the name of a structuralist – influenced literary theory. However, Wellek always emphasized the importance of interpretation in literary criticism and was impatient with purely empirical approaches to literary scholarship.

From the 1950's onwards, France became the centre for both structuralism and structuralist semiotics. In contrast to Prague, however, no single homogeneous movement was created in Paris. Jakobson's influence was also felt upon the work of French literary theorist and semiotician, Roland Barthes (1915 – 1980), who tried to expose how bourgeois society used signs to impose cultural values through fashion. Barthes explained that these bourgeois cultural myths were second – order signs, or connotations. For instance, the portrayal of wine drinking in French society was, at the time, presented as a healthy habit, something which contradicted reality. Marketing will contribute to create new signifiers which in turn created new signifieds. In 1952, Barthes settled at the Centre National de la Recherche Scientifique, where he studied lexicology and sociology. He began to write a popular series of bi – monthly essays for the magazine *Les Lettres Nouvelles*, in which he dismantled myths of popular culture (gathered in the *Mythologies* collection that was published in 1957). Barthes spent the early 1960s exploring the fields of semiology and structuralism, chairing various faculty positions around France, and continuing to produce more full – length studies. During this time, he wrote his best – known work, the 1967 essay "The Death of the Author", which, in light of the growing influence of Jacques Derrida's deconstruction, and continued to contribute with Philippe Sollers to the avant – garde literary magazine *Tel Quel*.

French semiotician Algirdas Julien Greimas (1917 – 1992) developed the branch of semiotics known as narratology, which he defined as the study of how human beings in different cultures invent similar kinds of narratives (myths, tales, etc.) with virtually the same stock of characters, motifs, themes, and plots. Greimas explores those codes that Barthes sees as outside of the mere forward temporal progression of narrative, that is, the symbolic, semantic, and cultural codes (rather than the proairetic and hermeneutic codes, according to Barthes' categories). Greimas "influences in understanding the deep structure of narrative include Vladimir Propp's exploration of the deep structure of folklore in *Morphology of the Folktale* and Claude Lévi – Strauss" work on the structure of myth. Greimas seeks the underlying grammar of narrative, "the semiolinguistic nature of the categories used in setting up these [narratological] models" (1976: 63). He wishes to find behind any "manifestation of narrativity" a "*fundamental semantics and grammar*" (1976: 65). Greimas is also interested in extending the relevance of narratology to all experience. He wishes to find the deep structures by which all signification orders the world of perception. As Greimas puts it, "From this perspective the sensible world as a whole becomes the object of the quest for signification. As long as it takes on form, the world appears, as a whole and in its various articulations, as potential meaning. Signification can be concealed *behind* all sensible phenomena; it is present behind sounds, but also behind images, odors, and flavors, without being in sounds or in images (as perceptions)" (1976: 63).

Originally from Lithuania, the family settled in Paris where in 1944 he enrolled for graduate study at the Sorbonne. In 1965 he became professor at the École des Hautes Études en Sciences Sociales (EHESS) in Paris where he taught for almost 25 years. He co – founded and became Secretary General of the International Association for Semiotic Studies. Greimas developed a structural version of semiotics named *generative semiotics*, trying to shift the focus of discipline from signs to systems of signification. He also characterized the sign as a four – component relational structure, whereby we understand the meaning of a specific sign (i. e. rich) by relating it to its opposites (i. e. not rich/poor). For Saussure and his structuralist followers, linguistic units do not have an identity as such, their presence is defined by their opposites, that is, by absences, as poststructural criticism noted.

According to Greimas, any narrative is merely a manifestation of such deep structures: "narrative forms are no more than particular organizations of the semiotic form of the content for which the theory of narration attempts to account" (1976: 114). For Greimas, a single word entails a limited a family of related terms which takes signification across a narrative. For example, the *sun* organizes around itself a figural field that includes *rays*, *light*, *heat*, *air*, *transparency*, *opacity*, *clouds*, etc. (1976: 115). Thus, the structural oppositions implied in symbols, characters or themes can be traced in the words used. Greimas argues that we can posit a structural relation between a given narrative's characters (narrative structures) and themes (discursive structures): "A character in a novel, supposing that it is introduced by the attribution of a name conferred on it, is progressively created by consecutive figurative notations extending throughout the length of the text, and it does not exist as a complete figure until the last page, thanks to the cumulative memorizing of the reader" (1976: 119). For Greimas, "An actor is... a meeting point and locus of conjunction for narrative structures and discursive structures, for the grammatical and the semantic components" (1976: 120). Greimas started from the following assumptions: a) culture has an axiological and ideological character; b) culture is not a ref lection of nature; c) there exists a "pre – code" which generates the homogeneous process of cultural production. Thus, for Greimas, the mechanism responsible for the functioning of culture is a structure defining the arrangement of signifying elements, that is, narrative. Like Propp, Greimas sought to develop a theoretical tool that made it theoretically possible to generate all possible texts. As Barthes notes, for the structuralist "the first task is to divide up narrative and... define the smallest narrative units... Meaning must be the criterion of the unit: it is the functional nature of certain segments of the story that makes them units—hence the name, functions immediately attributed to these first units" (Barthes 1977: 88).

In 1928 Vladimir Propp, a Russian folklorist published *Morphology of the Folktale*. Morphology is the study of forms—that is, the component parts of something and their relationships to each other and to the whole. Propp explained his work as follows:

> We are undertaking a comparison of the themes of these tales. For the sake of comparison we shall separate the component parts offairy tales by special methods; and then, we shall make a comparison of the tales according to their components. The result will be a morphology (i. e., a description of the tale according to its component parts and the relationship of these components to each other and to the whole) (1928: 19).

Propp refers to the essential or basic narrative unit in his study as a "function", "understood as an act of a character, defined from the point of view of its significance for the course of the action" (1928: 21) . In this sense, a) functions of characters constitute the fundamental components of a tale and serve as stable elements; b) the number of functions in fairy tales is limited; c) the sequence of functions is always the same; d) all fairy tales are of one type in regard to their structure. Propp interpreted a hundred fairy tales in terms of around 30 functions. Such functions are basic units of action. He listed seven *roles*: the *villain*, the *donor*, the *helper*, the *sought – for – person* (*and her father*), the *dispatcher*, the *hero* and the *false hero* and schematized the various "functions" within the story as follows (reproduced in Chandler 2007: 90).

As Barthes noted, "the first analysts of narrative were attempting... to see all the world's stories... within a single structure" and that this was a task which was "ultimately undesirable, for the text thereby loses its difference" (Barthes, 1974: 3). Indeed, the issue of re – establishing "difference" lies behind poststructural criticism. The theoretical advances made during this period concerned two apparently heterogeneous areas: on the one hand the search for an elementary structure of meaning comprising the logical classification of paradigmatic differences, and on the other, formulating a theory of narrativity which streamlined Propp's syntagmatic model into the components of a narrative grammar. During

1	Initial Situation	Members of family of hero introduced
2	Absentation	One of the members absents himself from home
3	Interdiction	An interdiction is addressed to the hero
4	Violation	An interdiction is violated
5	Reconnaissance	The villain makes an attempt at reconnaissance
6	Delivery	The villain receives information about his victim
7	Trickery	The villain attempts to deceive the victim
8	Complicity	The victim submits to deception, unwittingly helps his enemy
9	Villainy	The villain causes harm or injury to members of the family
10	Lack	One member of a family lacks something or wants something
11	Mediation	Misfortune is known. Hero is dispatched
12	Counteraction	Seekers decide to agree on counteraction
13	Departure	The hero leaves home
14	1st function of donor	Hero is tested, receives magical agent donor or helper
15	Hero's Reaction	Hero reacts to action of the future donor
16	Receipt of Magic Agent	Hero acquires the use of magical agent
17	Spatial Transference	Hero is led to object of search
18	Struggle	Hero and villain join in direct combat
19	Branding	Hero is branded
20	Victory	Villain is defeated
21	Liquidation	Initial misfortune or lack is liquidated
22	Return	The hero returns
23	Pursuit	A chase: the hero is pursued
24	Rescue	Rescue of hero from pursuit
25	Unrecognized	The hero, unrecognized, arrives home or in another arrival country
26	Unfounded claims	A false hero presents unfounded claims
27	Difficult task	A difficult task is proposed to the hero
28	Solution	The task is resolved
29	Recognition	The hero is recognized
30	Exposure	The false hero or villain is exposed
31	Transfiguration	The hero is given a new appearance
32	Punishment	The villain is punished
33	Wedding	The hero is married and ascends the throne

the second phase of semiotic research, in the 1970s, attempts were made to find a synthesis between these different fields in order to define a consistent general theory of the generation of meaning. Concentrating on the surface structures of narrative, semioticians discovered that function, as represented by an action verb, was overdetermined by modalities: two virtualizing (wanting, having to) and two actualizing (knowing how to, being able to). When this discovery was pushed to its extremes, it emerged that the entire narrative grammar was in fact composed merely of modalities plus content, that is, semantics. The new models could also be applied to social practices, behaviour patterns, etc. Narrativity was no longer seen to be the exclusive property of written texts. From now on it was perceived as underlying all discourse. Greimas also proposed a visual representation of the elementary structure of meaning: the semiotic square. This is the logical expression of any semantic category showing all possible relationships that define it, i. e. opposition, contradiction and implication. It was discovered, however, that apart from illustrating opposing relationships, this square also portrays the operations they generate. In fact, it allows to retrace a process in progress or the trajectory of a subject performing acts of transformation (Greimas and Courtes, 1979). During the 1980s and 1990s, efforts concentrated in particular on the spatial, temporal and actorial organization of texts, but none of this took into consideration the question of external reference nor the belief in the existence of a single reality independent of its linguistic articulation, which was thought be a symptom of futile empiricism. In S/Z, Barthes was the first to assume that the deep structure of the literary work could be presented within the surface structure, by dividing the work into "units of reading" (lexia). He applied this technique to *Saracine* by Honore de Balzac in order to prove that the realism of this novel was questionable. In *La Struttura Assente*, Eco came to the conclusion that because of its concerns with the replication of inner units, structuralism was unable to generate a theory of the artistic avant – garde (303 – 320).

The French philosopher of language Jacques Derrida (1930 – 2004) criticized the suppression of the materiality of the sign, the neglect of cultural aspects, and the existence of dualities (oppositions), such as primacy of the spoken word over the written. In *Of Grammatology*, Derrida's revised the conceptions of language and art, from Plato to the contemporary structural anthropologist Claude Levi – Strauss, in order to show how the spoken word had held a privileged position in the Western worldview, being regarded as intimately involved in our sense of self and constituting a sign of truth and authenticity. Speech had become so thoroughly naturalized that the signifier becomes equivalent to that which it represents, becoming almost impossible to trace, almost erasing itself. Derrida also argued that the written sign was gradually constructed in parallel to the ethical (dual) notions of truth and authenticity (built in contrast to their opposites). Although Lévi – Strauss had set the basis of the importance of materiality in his conception of "bricolage", which sought to show how the process of creation involves a dialogue with the materials and means of execution, suggesting the course of action and the methodology to follow, to Derrida, this was not enough. In seeking to establish "Grammatology" or the study of textuality, Derrida championed the primacy of the material dimension so that the materiality of a word cannot be translated or carried over into another language.

Thus, he argued that in the Western world, the influence of Descartes' *Cogito ergo sum* (I think therefore I am) can still be felt in any theory of knowledge and language. He describes this as "metaphysics of presence", which means that the speaking/thinking subject always speaks from a position of making himself/herself "present" to consciousness. Thus, the notion of meaning takes the form of something present (notice the expression "to have in mind") to the consciousness of the speaker at the moment of the utterance. Derrida makes this clear in view of Saussure's emphasis on oral discourse and his neglect of written language. Indeed, in order to be able to identify a spoken sound, one need to attend to the moment of the utterance itself, and its recording, whether in written speech or in any other form of sound capture, creates a gap, where signifier and signified cannot meet. Only in the spoken moment signified and signifier are together, with the physical and the mental perfectly fused. This moment of "presence", according to Derrida serves as a point of reference to establish a relation of "unity", against which all other points of difference, of distinction, are posited. In Derrida's words:

> The system of s' entendre parler through the phonic substance—which presents it-
> self as the non – exterior, non – mundane. and therefore non – empirical or contingent
> signifier—has necessarily dominated the history of the world during an entire epoch, and
> has even produced the idea of the world, the idea of world – origin, that arises from the
> difference between the worldly and the non – worldly, the outside and the inside, ideality
> and non – ideality, universal and non – universal, transcendental and empirical, etc.
> (1976: 7 – 8).

Grammatology, according to Derrida, is not an alternative methodology,
but the "name" of a question (1972: 22), or rather "a name". Indeed,
Derrida's own writing involves a series of strategic manoeuvres and displacements
in which he modifies his terms, producing a chain of related but non – identical
operators, *differance*, supplement, trace, *pharmakon*, to prevent any of his terms
from becoming universal "concepts". Thus, while structuralism sought to find
universal patterns of analysis (metalanguages), poststructuralism tends to view
communication as a process, more in line with Peirce's model.

Even if there is no outside language, as Derrida would say, communication
still depends on multiple media formats, from biophysical to technological.
Awareness of this fact has come hand in hand with the use of new materials in architecture, the visual and other arts, and a desire for syncretism shown, for instance, in 20 th – century avant – garde. It was Umberto Eco who is responsible
for one of the broadest definitions, who states that "semiotics is concerned with
everything that can be taken as a sign" (1979: 3). In this way, contemporary
semiotics explores the evolution of codes in different cultural systems that make
sense of the world in different ways.

The 1980s and 1990s saw the growth of postmodernism but also of cultural
semiotics. unable to find an academic position in Leningrad due to anti – Semitism
Juri Lotman (1922 – 1993) went to Estonia in 1950 and from 1954 began his
work as a lecturer at the Department of Russian language and literature of Tartu
University, where he later founded of the Moscow – Tartu school of cultural se-

miotics. Lotman developed a semiotic approach to the study of culture and established a communication model for the study of text semiotics, introducing the concept of the semiosphere to refer to the semiotic space of culture (Lotman, 1990: 124 – 125) which is not mapped in territorial terms, having to do with political and economic units such as the Estate or the Nation. Instead, it offers a dynamic vision of cultural semiosis which considers the interaction of different semiotic structures and their socio – cultural functioning. These structures encompass changing media channels and technologies, from print to photography to radio, TV and cinema, each using diverse technologies for text, image or sound recording and broadcasting. Among Lotman's colleagues was Vladimir Toporov.

Norman Fairclough also argued that the differences in media channels and technologies had an impact on the communication and interpersonal relationships enabled by each media channel. For instance, he contemplated radio as foregrounded through the transmission of the individual qualities of a person's voice, which television made even more visible in movement and action (Fairclough, 1995: 38–9). Thus, while human experiences are inherently multisensory, every representation of experience is subject to the constraints and affordances of the medium involve and by the channels which the medium uses, as Christian Metz (1931 – 1993) also argued. The term medium includes association with different forms of text support, whether biophysical, for instance oral speech, or technological, including print (with text, images/photos and so on), broadcasting in mass media (radio, TV, cinema etc.), involving various channels (visual, auditory, tactile etc.), and different technologies (telephone, fax, e-mail, video conferencing, computer – based chat systems).

Thomas A. Sebeok (1920—2001) has argued that the concept of modelling system, put forth by the Moscow – Tartu School, has been central to semiotics since the 1960s, but that it has derived from structural linguistic study and only focused on cultural aspects to the exclusion of the rest of nature. Thus, Sebeok has put forth a wider conception of semiotics that includes other biological organisms. Sebeok was born in Budapest (Hungary) and became resident in the

United States in 1941. Sebeok earned a bachelor's degree and a masters in 1945 at the University of Chicago and a doctorate at Princeton University. He then taught at Indiana University in Bloomington, establishing in 1969, the journal "Semiotica". Sebeok insisted that all communication was made possible by the relationship between an organism and the environment it lives in, and posed the equation between semiosis (the activity of interpreting signs) and life—the view that has further developed by Copenhagen—Tartu Biosemiotic School. To Peirce's classification of signs, Sebeok added the symptom and the signal. For Peirce , the symptom was never a distinct species of sign , but a mere subspecies, namely the index (Peirce, CP 2 : 304 &8: 119) Symptoms, in Peirce's usage , are thus indexes, interpretable by their receivers without the actuality of any intentional sender. Likewise, Jakobson includes symptoms within the scope of semiotics (1971: 703) Symptoms like increased heart rate, pain, nausea, hunger, thirst, and the like, are private experiences; they tend to be signified by paraphonetic means, such as groans or verbal signs, which may or may not be coupled with gestures. Thus, symptoms generally precede signs, which is to say that the orderly unfolding of evidence may be termed prognostic (Sebeok, 1994: 80).

Sebeok explains thatthe symptom is "a compulsive , automatic, non – arbitrary sign" (Sebeok, 1994: 46), a reflex of anatomical structure, often extended metaphorically to refer to intellectual, emotional, and social phenomena that result from causes that are perceived to be analogous to physical processes. (Sebeok, 1994: 9). "Le symptom, ce serait le reel apparent ou l' apparent reel" (Barthes, 1972 : 38, Sebeok, 1994: 47) Semiotics, referring in earliest usage to medical concerns with the sensible indications of changes in the condition of the human body—constituted one of the three branches of Greek medicine. Since symptoms were among the earliest signs identified, they constitute, according to Sebeok, a historically important category for any inquiry into the beginnings of the theory of signs. Sebeok mentions how Barthes (1972) assigns the symptom to the category that Hjelmslev called "substance" (versus form / expression versus content) of the signifier, only with regards to clinical discourse. For Sebeok, the symptom includes signs by a speechless creature, for instance, as in the case of autonomic displays described by Charles Darwin with regards to intraspecific animal communication; a sort of reflex action, independent of will. One example would be sweating from fear, pain or anger. Another example is the production of saliva, or high temperature when the organism is ill.

Sebeok explains that animals have an innate capacity to use and respond to species—specific signals for survival, and that most signals are emitted automatically in response to specific types of stimuli and affective states. A large portion of bodily communication among humans also unfolds largely in the form of signals. For example, particular physical features play an important role in sexual attraction. Humans are capable as well of deploying witting signals for some intentional purpose, for instance, nodding, winking, glancing, looking, nudging, kicking, head tilting (Sebeok, 1994: 10; 44). Sebeok's argument is based on Peirce's own description of semiosis: all dynamical action, or action by brute force, physical or psychical, either takes place between two subjects ... or at any rate is a resultant of such actions between pairs. But by "semiosis" I mean, on the contrary, an action, or influence, which is, or involves, a co-operation of three subjects, such as a sign, its object, and its interpretant, this tri-relative inf luence not being in any way resolvable into actions between pairs... my definition confers on anything that so acts the title of a "sign" (Peirce, 5 : 484; Sebeok, 1994: 45 –6) .

Sebeok also mentioned the importance of nonverbal communication, which takes place within an organism or between two or more organisms. Within an organism, participators in communicative acts may involve cellular organelles, cells, tissues, organs, and organ systems, including processes such as protein synthesis, metabolism, hormone activity, the transmission of nervous impulses and so on (Sebeok, 1994: 12). Because of his interest in biosemiotics, Sebeok has been one of the first semioticians to pay attention to material aspects of communication, explaining, for example, the functioning of the "channel". He explains that animals communicate through different channels or combinations of media. "Any form of energy propagation can, in fact, be exploited for purposes of message transmission" explains Sebeok (1994: 14). Sound is the most extended modality of communication among many animals, including humans. Insects, for instance, which outnumber the rest of animals, use sound widely (for example, grasshoppers, mantises, cockroaches, coleoptera, beetles and so on) and have complex sound – producing mechanisms and hearing organs on the forepart of their abdomen. Sebeok indicates that it is useful to distinguish not only nonverbal from verbal but also nonvocal from vocal communication. The vocal mechanism that works by means of air passing over the vocal cords, setting them into vibration, seems to be confined to humans, other mammals, birds, some reptiles, and amphibians. Verbal but not vocal language is used in some North and South American Indian sign languages, Australian aboriginal sign languages, and monastic communication systems (where silence is a rule of the religious congregation). It is also use in miming, pantomime theatre or some varieties of ballet. Other unvoiced sign languages are used for secrecy and in rituals. Sometimes nonverbal acoustic messages—with or without speech—are used behind masks, inanimate figures, such as puppets or marionettes, or through other performing objects (Sebeok, 1994: 14 – 16).

Non – verbal communication involves smells (olfaction, odour, scent, aroma) Smell is used for purposes of communication crucially, by sharks and hedgehogs, social insects such as bees, termites, and ants, and such social mammals as wolves and lions. It is less important in birds and primates, which rely largely on sight. Smell are also associated with sexual behavior (Sebeok, 1994: 20). Gestures, dance and other forms of performance are also important in animal mating protocols. "Facial expressions—pouting, the curled lip, a raised eyebrow, crying, flaring nostrils—constitute a powerful , universal communication system, solo or in concert. Eye work, including gaze and mutual gaze, can be particularly powerful in understanding arange of quotidian vertebrate as well as human social behaviour" (Sebeok, 1994: 21). The study of spatial and temporal bodily arrangements is called "proxemics" .

Umberto Eco (1932 –) also extended Peirce's classification of "iconic signs" to which he purposes four modes of sign production: recognition, ostension, replica, and invention (*A theory of semiotics*, *La struttura assente*, *Le signe*, *La production de signes*). The three trichotomies included: the sign—also called a *representamen*—which stands for something understood to be analogous to Saussure's signifier; a second sign is the *object* of the first sign—similar to the signified but with a non – specific quality of Platonic idealism; and a third sign, the *interpretant* posits the possibility of infinite associations between the first sign and its object (Peirce, 1955: 98 – 104;). Eco argues that the "interpretant" can be understood as a sign that refers to another sign or "conceived as the *definition* of the representamen" (Eco, 1976: 68). The interpretant, then, is another sign referring to itself in a cycle where meaning can be deferred endlessly. Thus "the very definition of 'sign' implies a process of *unlimited semiosis*" (Eco, 1976: 69) . Thus, the process of semiosis or signification may produce a variety of meanings from the same sign. Eco is founder of the Dipartimento di Comunicazione at the University of San Marino, President of the *Scuola Superiore di Studi Umanistici*, University of Bologna. He was one of the pioneers of "Reader Response Criticism". In 1962 he published *Opera aperta* (translated into English as "The Open Work") where he argued that literary texts are fields of meaning, rather than strings of meaning, that they are understood as open, internally dynamic and psychologically engaging. Eco emphasizes the fact that words do not have meanings that are simply lexical, but rather, they operate in the context of utterance. As Eco puts it: "Codes and subcodes are applied to the message [read 'text'] in the light of a general framework of cultural references, which constitutes the receiver's patrimony of knowledge: his ideological, ethical, religious standpoints, his psychological attitudes, his tastes, his value systems, etc. " The Italian semiotician offers some examples that suggest how such aberrant decodings might have taken place in the past: foreigners in strange cultures who do not know the codes, or people who interpret messages in terms of their own codes rather than the codes in which the messages were originally cast. This was, Eco notes, before the development of mass media, when aberrant decodings were the exception, not the rule. With the development of mass media, however, the situation changed radically, and aberrant decoding became the norm. According to Eco, this is because of the wide gap that exists between those who create and generate the material carried by the media and those who receive this material.

Bulgarian Julia Kristeva (1941) was the first translator of the work of Russian scholar Mikhail Bakhtin (1895 – 1975) into the West, developing his concept of "intertextuality" and "dialogism". Bakhtin made clear that literary texts were always dialogic in relation to readers and audiences, and that literary discourse proceeds only by referencing, quoting, assuming an other's speech or words. The reader/audience is therefore always already inscribed in the medium/message/text/visual sign. Discourses, texts, cultural message presuppose and embody a network of implicit references, gestures, an unmarked quotations from other works. Bakhtin is also credited with the definition of intertextuality. He saw literary discourse and individual literary texts as an intersection of multiple textual surfaces rather than as a fixed point or meaning, that is, as a dialogue among various texts, genres, and voices: the writer's, the character's, the historical cultural context, the readers'/audiences'. To Bakhtin, each statement in a discourse, each expression in a text, is an intersection of words or texts where at least one other word or text can be read. Discourse thus can be described as having a horizontal axis, composed of the writer, characters (in a novel), and genre being written, and the vertical axis, composed of the text and its context in a larger universe of discourses, texts, meanings, values. Any text, therefore, is always at least double, presupposing, incorporating, and transforming other voices. Bakhtin contributed to show how the boundary lines between someone else's speech and one's own speech were f lexible, ambiguous, and could be deliberately distorted (one of Bakhtin's areas of study was parody). Texts were constructed like mosaics out of the texts of others, a "history of appropriation, re – working and imitation of someone else's property" (1981: 69) .

Kristeva studied at the University of Sofia and obtained a fellowship at the Sorbonne in 1965. She established herself in Paris where she worked with the structuralist and Marxist critic Lucien Goldmann, the social and literary critic Roland Barthes, and the structuralist anthropologist Claude Lévi – Strauss. She soon became a member of the group of intellectuals associated with the journal *Tel Quel*, founded by Philippe Sollers whom she married in 1967. Kristeva earned a degree in Psychoanalysis in 1979 and her research tries to merge this with semiotics. For Kristeva, the semiotic is a realm associated with the musical, the poetic, the rhythmic, and that which lacks structure and meaning, representing the undifferentiated state of the Lacanian pre-Mirror Stage infant. She also relates semiotics to a feminine understanding of communication, signalling the difference between the more masculine symbolic realm (the symbolic refers here to Lacan's conception). Upon entering the Mirror Stage, the child learns to distinguish between self and other, and enters the realm of shared cultural meaning, known as the symbolic. In *Desire in Language* (1980) , Kristeva describes the symbolic as the space in which the development of language allows the child to become a "speaking subject", and to develop a sense of identity separate from the mother. This process of separation is known as abjection, whereby the child must reject and move away from the mother in order to enter into the world of language, culture, meaning, and the social. This realm of language is called the symbolic and is contrasted with the semiotic in that it is associated with the masculine, the law and structure. Kristeva departs from Lacan in the idea that even after entering the symbolic, the subject continues to oscillate between the semiotic and the symbolic.

In *Revolution in Poetic Language* (1974) and *Polylogue* (1977) , Kristeva theorizes the constitution of the subject by distinguishing between the semiotic and symbolic modalities of the signifying process. These modalities are relatively exclusive and necessarily dialectical. This distinction is established through the subtle combination of concepts drawn from the later works of Plato and from psychoanalytic, phenomenological, and linguistic theories. Semiotic processes predate the symbolic ones and are instinctual and maternal. They are unregulated but ordered according to biological and social constraints, as well as by drives organized around the mother's body. Kristeva uses the concept of *chora* to describe the continuous rhythmic and feminine space shared by mother and child prior to the emergence of what she calls the *thetic* phase that prepares the sign for emergence into the symbolic order. In the thetic phase, the subject is on the threshold of language. Kristeva sets out the phenomenological description of the thesis by positing existence through propositions that are the foundation of signification. Kristeva then subjects descriptions of intentionality, judgment, the constitution of objects, and predicative syntheses derived from studies of the transcendental ego to a genetic psychoanalytic perspective, enlisting both the mirror stage of Jacques Lacan and the castration complex of Sigmund Freud. Thetic consciousness is essentially a two – sided intentional structure of constitutive acts and objects in which the transcendental ego belongs and is revealed in operations of predication and judgment. For Kristeva, the speaking subject is a "split unification" of conscious and unconscious levels, of semiotic and symbolic dispositions. Psychoanalysis functions for Kristeva as a way to dislodge the transcendental ego and the overinvestment in consciousness and reason and as a way to investigate the signifying process at work on both the conscious and, especially, the unconscious sides of the speaking subject. Unlike thetic consciousness, the speaking subject is not sequestered by the phenomenological reduction from the social constraints of family, modes of production, the unconscious, and the body, all of which support signifying practices, beyond the single support of meaning provided by the transcendental ego.

Semiotic processes disrupt the symbolic domain of meaning and significance described as paternal, rational and transcendental. The semiotic breaks into the symbolic through a transgressive breach, exploding the unity of transcendental consciousness. The symbolic is best taken in terms of the oppositional interdependencies across the field of language and culture, understood in the structural sense developed by Lacan and Claude Lévi – Strauss. Language presupposes both modalities in the engendering of the speaking subject, but Kristeva uses the semiotic to develop an analysis capable of accounting for instinctual drives, which explains her heavy reliance on a variety of psychoanalytic theories. Kristeva's goal is to overcome the debt linguistics has to phenomenology, in which the transcendental ego sustains signification by disembodying heterogeneous drives of the unconscious. Still, semiotic phenomena tend to establish quasi-symbolic signifying apparatuses in order to communicate, even if what is communicated is undecidable and indeterminate; without them, however, discourse goes mad. It is for this reason that Kristeva allows that heterogeneous semiotic processes remain near the thetic.

In terms of the functioning of texts, Kristeva defines a text's genotext as a nonlinguistic, semiotic processuality that articulates ephemeral structures and is heterogeneous to meaning. The phenotext, in contrast, denotes language that is in the service of univocity and is obedient to the rules of communication. It is thus homogeneous with meaning and the direct passage of univocal information between subjects and does not wander like the genotext does. The grammatical and syntactical deviations of the genotext may be seen at work in certain experimental literary practices such as James Joyce's *Finnegans Wake* and in revolutionary periods during which the structure of the phenotext is modified.

For Kristeva, semiotics is limited by its subservience to linguistics and the homogenizing reduction of signifying practices to a system. Semiotics cannot, then, identify the heterogeneous operations of the signifying process. The goal of Kristevan "semanalysis", then is to include both the genotext and the phenotext in the study of signifying practices. Toward this goal, the phenomenological reduction must be demystified, leading to the liberation of the speaking subject and its reconnection with socio and biohistorical factors. Semanalysis is materialist, in non – Hegelian and non – Marxist senses, in that it develops a topology rather than an algebra of the signifying practices of a subject in process.

In avant – garde art, Kristeva sees semiotic operations that she identifies with what she calls the polylogical subject. The polylogue is primally musical and material. It is the rhythm of the unconscious before it is repressed and dematerialized in a signifying system. It is also the presyntactic enunciations of the child and the psychotic operating before and outside of the confines of the symbolic network. The polylogue forces language out of the transcendental position by means of multiplication and breaks through the boundaries of the symbolic by means of what Kristeva calls the transfinite element of language, which goes beyond the sentence and naming. Kristeva privileges the study of the languages of children and psychotics because they reveal in concomitant ways the entrances to and exits from the symbolic order of language and sociality.

Finally, *Powers of Horror* (1982) theorizes the space between the semiotic and the symbolic and between subject and object by using the concept of the abject, which defines the boundaries around the subject in terms of what is cast out and rendered other. The concept essentially concerns the problematic corporeality of the subject, which the symbolic order seeks to transcend. The symbolic subject's abjection of what is improper, unclean, and defiling is a requirement that is never accomplished with any finality. The object is never fully other, since it was once part of the subject, and so it dwells on the unclear border between subject and object, thus threatening the subject's need to master it and distinguish itself from it. Bodily waste must be excreted so that the subject's body may continue to live, yet eventually the body itself becomes waste, a corpse. But the corpse is ambiguous because it can no longer be maintained as the subject's location, nor is it solely an object. The corpse is the future of every embodied subject. Kristeva's example of the corpse shows how the abject shifts the border between life and death into life, revealing a necessary relation that the symbolic order can tolerate only through repression.

Kristeva's contribution to social semiotics has been criticized by Gayatri Chakravorty Spivak and Ian Almond (2007: 154 – 5) as ethnocentric, particularly in what refers Kristeva's volume on Chinese women (1977). Such criticisms show the need for cross – cultural approaches that integrate and try to make sense of diverse visions on the semiotic study of communication and representation using more complex paradigms and taking into consideration different languages and different forms of materiality.

To conclude, this chapter has presented an overview of the semiotic panorama in the West. I have attempted to show how the notion of sign has open itself to incorporate various materialities as well as perspectives from various disciplines. Initially, the term text referred to the message, an assemblage of signs such as words, images, sounds and/or gestures. When recorded in some way (e. g. writing, audio- and video-recording), the message became physically independent from sender and receiver. Semioticians have commonly referred to films, television and radio programs, advertising posters and so on as "texts", functioning like natural "languages", forcing all media into a linguistic framework.

Historical evidence indicates a tendency of linguistic signs to evolve from indexical and iconic forms towards symbolic forms. Peirce also notedthat signs were "originally in part iconic, in part indexical" and he adds that "in all primitive writing, such as Egyptian hieroglyphics, there are icons of a non – logical kind, the ideographs" so that "in the earliest form of speech there probably was a large element of mimicry" (CP 2. 280). Over time, linguistic signs would have developed a more symbolic and conventional character which can be seen in the evolution of Western alphabets. In China, however, writing has retained a strong iconic and indexical component, as it can be seen in chapter four of this volume. This shift from the iconic to the symbolic may have been dictated by the economy of using a chisel or a brush.

Because the medium is not neutral, each materiality, each technology has its own constraints and is charged with cultural significations (Eco, 1976: 267). For instance, photographic and audio – visual media are almost invariably regarded as more real than other forms of representation because of their emphasis on iconic and indexical properties. Working in the field of visual semiotics, Gunther Kress and Theovan Leeuwen have defended that "the material expression of the text is always significant; it is a separately variable semiotic feature" and that changing the signifier at the level of form, or its materiality and medium, impacts directly on the signified (Kress & van Leeuwen, 1996: 231).

After the 1990s, the conversion of analogue formats in digitalization, has brought the inquiry into thedifferent types of interactional communicative behavior into a new era of semiotics. In their 1998 book entitled *Remediation*, Jay David Bolter and Richard Grusin argued that the more frequently and fluently a medium is used, the more "transparent" to its users it tends to become. The term "remediation" refers to the conversion of content from one medium to another, including not just forms of adaptation (for example from a novel to a film) but changes involving the inclusion of different codes (for instance in digital communication we have not just analogic codes —those used in natural languages— but also mathematical codes, such as binary code and other forms of algorithmic programing. Analogical signs (such as visual images, gestures, textures, tastes and smells) involve graded relationships on a continuum.

Digitalization has also shown that it is fundamentally impossible to draw complete "analogies" between analogic and digital media, as the codes they employ are different and function differently. The final result might converted into the cognitive organizing principles related to perception (seeing, hearing, touch and so on), so that we are able to process the information on the computer or cell – phone screens, for instance, but the algorithmic programming behind the screen conditions the way we interact with this information. For instance, in text – processing programs, such as word, we might be able to do online cut-paste, and include some fixed images. However, for images to be in movement, other formats have to be used (i. e. gif). Thus, the medium influences and conditions the way the receptor "uses" information without being fully aware of this. This phenomenon was first pointed out by media theorist Marshall McLuhan in his famous aphorism "The medium is the massage", playing with the word "message" and changing it to suggest the hidden purpose behind each media. Thus, the materiality of signs affect power relations in communication in general, and in cross-cultural communication in particular.

REFERENCES

［1］ Aquinas Thomas. In Aristotelis Librum de Anima Commentarium. c. 1266 – 1272. Ed. A. M. Pirotta. Turin: Marietti, 1948.

［2］ Almond Ian. The New Orientalists: Postmodern Representations of Islam from Foucault to Baudrillard, I. B. Tauris, 2007.

［3］ Aristotle. The works of Aristotle. Vol. I. Categoriae, De interpretatione, Analytica priora, Analytica posteriora, Topica and de Sophisticis elenchis. English translation by W. D. Ross. Oxford: Clarendon Press, 1937.

［4］ Augustine. De Doctrina Christiana c. 397 – 426. English trans. by D. W. Robertson. India napolis: Bobbs – Merrill, 1977.

［5］ Bakhtin Mikhail. Problemy poetiki Dostoevskogo, Leningrad 1929. Trans. as Problems of Dostoevsky's Poetics by R. W. Rotsel. Ann Arbor, MI: Ardis, 1973, and by Caryl Emerson. Minneapolis, MN: University of Minnesota Press, 1984.

［6］ Bakhtin Mikhail. Voprosy literatury i estetiki ［M］ //. Trans. Caryl Emerson and Michael Holquist as The Dialogic Imagination; Four Essays by M. M. Bakhtin, Ed. Michael Holquist. Austin: University of Texas Press, 1981.

［7］ Barthes Mythologies. Paris, Editions du Seuil, 1957. Translated by Annette Lavers in London, Paladin, 1972 and by Richard Howard in New York, Hill & Wang, 1979.

［8］ Barthes Roland. Elements de Sémiologie. Paris: Seuil, 1964. Trans. by Annette Lavers and Colin Smith as Elements of Semiology. New York: Hill and Wang, 1967.

［9］ Barthes Roland. Système de la mode, Editions du Seuil: Paris, 1967.

［10］ Barthes Roland. L'Empire des signes, Skira: Paris, 1970.

［11］ Barthes Roland. S/Z, Seuil: Paris, 1970.

［12］ Barthes Roland. Le Degré zéro de l'écriture suivi de Nouveaux essais critiques, Editions du Seuil: Paris, 1972. Writing degree zero and elements of semiology. Translated by A. Lavers & C. Smith. Boston: Beacon.

［13］ Barthes Roland. Le plaisir du texte ［M］ Editions du Seuil: Paris, 1973.

［14］ Berkeley George. Alciphron, or The Minute Philosopher. 1732. In The Works of George Berkeley, Bishop of Cloyne. Ed. T. Jessop Vol. III. London: Thomas Nelson and Sons, 1950.

［15］ Bouissac Paul. Saussure's legacy in semiotics ［M］. The Cambridge Companion to Saussure. Ed. Carol Sanders. Cambridge University Press, 2004.

[16] Burke Kenneth. The Philosophy of Literary Form, Studies in Symbolic Action [M]. Baton Rouge, 1941.

[17] Castañares, Wenceslao. Lines of Development of Greek Semiotics [J]. Special Issue on Semiotics of Culture. Cultura: Journal of Philosophy and Axiology of Culture. 2012 (9.2): 11 – 33.

[18] Chandler Daniel. Semiotics for beginners [M]. 2007. http: //www. aber. ac. uk/ media/Documents/S4B/

[19] Coseriu Eugen [M]. Sprache, Strukturen und Funktionen. Tübingen, 1970.

[20] Culler Jonathan. Ferdinand de Saussure [M]. New York: Penguin, 1977.

[21] Culler Jonathan. The Pursuit of Signs. Semiotics, Literature, Deconstruction [M]. Ithaca, NY: Cornell University Press. 1981. Bordieu, Pierre. (1991). Language & Symbolic Power, Harvard University Press.

[22] Culle, Jonathan. Structuralist poetics: Structuralism, linguistics and the study of literature [M]. Ithaca, NY: Cornell University Press, 1976.

[23] Danesi Marcel. Encyclopedic Dictionary of Semiotics, Media, and Communications [M]. Toronto: University of Toronto Press, 2000.

[24] Danesi Marcel. The Quest for Meaning: A Guide to Semiotic Theory and Practice [M]. Toronto: University of Toronto Press, 2007.

[25] Deely John. Basics of Semiotics [M]. Bloomington: Indiana University Press, 1990.

[26] Derrida Jacques. Speech and Phenomena and Other Essays on Husserl's Theory of Signs [M]. Evanston: Northwestern University Press, 1973.

[27] Derrida Jacques. Of Grammatology [M]. Trans. by Gayatri Chakravorty Spivak. Baltimore: Johns Hopkins University Press, 1976.

[28] Derrida Jacques. Writing and Difference [M]. Gayatri Chakravorty Spivak, trans. Chicago: University of Chicago Press, 1978.

[29] Eco Umberto. Trattato di semiotica generale [M]. 1975. A Theory of Semiotics, Bloomington: Indiana University Press, 1976.

[30] Eco Umberto. The Code: Metaphor or Interdisciplinary Category? [J]. Yale Italian Studies 1977 (1): 24 – 52.

[31] Eco Umberto. The Sign Revisited [J]. Philosophy and Social Criticism 73. 4 (1980): 263 – 297.

[32] Eco Umberto. On Symbols [J]. Recherche Sémiotique/Semiotic Inquiry, 1982 (2.1): 15 – 44.

[33] Eco Umberto. Semiotics and the Philosophy of Language [M] . Bloomington: Indiana University Press, 1984.

[34] Eco Umberto. Opera aperta [M] . 1976. English translation: The Open Work, 1989.

[35] Eco Umberto. Travels in Hyperreality [M] . Trans. William Weaver. New York: Harcourt, Brace, Jovanovich, 1986.

[36] Eco Umberto. The Role of the Reader: Explorations in the Semiotics of Texts [M] . Indiana University Press, 1979.

[37] Eagleton Terry. Literary Theory: and introduction [M] . University of Minnesota Press, 1983.

[38] Fiske Introduction to communication studies [M] . London: Routledge, 1982.

[39] Galen C. Opera Omnia [j] . Ed. C. G. Künh. Leipzig: Cnoblochii, vol. (20): 1821 – 1833.

[40] Greimas A. J. Structural Semantics: An Attempt at a Method [M] . Trans. Daniele McDowell, Ronald Schleifer, and Alan Velie. Lincoln, Nebraska: University of Nebraska Press, 1983.

[41] Greimas Algirdas Julian. On Meaning. Selected Writing in Semiotic Theory [M]. Trans. Paul J. Perron and Frank H. Collins. Minneapolis: University of Minnesota Press, 1976.

[42] Greimas Algirdas J. and Joseph Courtes. Semiotique, dictionnaire raisonne de la theorie du langage [M]. Paris: Hachette, 1979.

[43] Sexto Empírico. Sextus Empiricus in four volumes (Vol. 2), Against the logicians [M]. With an english translation by R. G. Bury. Cambridge, Massachusetts: Harvard University Press; London : William Heinemann, 1983.

[44] Hall Stuart. Encoding/Decoding [M] . Culture, Media, Language: Working Papers in Cultural Studies 1972 – 1979. Ed. Stuart Hall. London: Hutchinson.

[45] Harris Roy. Reading Saussure: A Critical Commentary on the "Cours de linguistique générale" [M] . London: Duckworth, 1987.

[46] Heidegger Martin. Sein und Zeit (1927), (10th) ed [M]. Tübingen: Niemeyer, 1963.

[47] Hippocrates. Ancient Medicine. With an english translation by W. H. S. Jones. London: Heinemann; Cambridge : Harvard University Press, 1972.

[48] Hippocrates. Pronostic [M] . With an english translation by W. H. S. Jones. London: Heinemann; Cambridge: Harvard University Press, vol II, 1967.

[49] Hippocrates. Prorrhetics [M] . With an English translation by P. Potter. London:

Heinemann; Cambridge: Harvard University Press, vol. VIII, 1995.

[50] Hjelmslev Louis. Prolegomena to a Theory of Language [M] . Translation by Francis J. Whitfield. Madison: University of Wisconsin Press, 1961.

[51] Hume David. An Enquiry concerning Human Understanding [M] //1748. Complete and unabridged text in The English Philosophers from Bacon to Mill. Ed. E. A. Burtt. New York: The Modern Library, 1939: 585 – 689.

[52] Jakobson Roman. and M. Halle. Fundamentals of Language [M] . The Hague: Mouton de Gruyter, 1956.

[53] Jakobson Roman. Coup d'oeil sur le devéloppement de la sémiotique [M] //Panorama Sémiotique/A Semiotic Landscape. Ed. Seymour Chatman, Umberto Eco, and Jean – Marie Klinkenberg. Proceedings of the International Association for Semiotic Studies, Milan, June 1974; The Hague: Mouton de Gruyter, 1979: 3 – 18.

[54] Jakobson Roman. Selected Writings (ed. Stephen Rudy) [M]. The Hague, Paris, Mouton, in six volumes (1971 – 1985) .

[55] Jameson Fredric. The Prison House of Language: A Critical Account of Structuralism and Russian Formalism [M]. Princeton: Princeton University Press, 1972.

[56] Kant, Immanuel. Kritik der reinen Vernunft [M]. 1781, 1787. English trans. by Norman Kemp Smith, Kant's Critique of Pure Reason. New York: St. Martin's Press, 1963.

[57] Kretzmann Norman. History of semantics [M] //Paul Edwards (ed.), The Encyclopedia of Philosophy, vol. 7, New York: Macmillan and The Free Press, 1967: 358 – 406.

[58] Kristeva, Julia. Séméiôtiké: recherches pour une sémanalyse, Paris: Edition du Seuil, 1969. Desire in Language: A Semiotic Approach to Literature and Art, Oxford: Blackwell, 1980.

[59] Kristeva Julia. La Révolution Du Langage Poétique: L'avant – Garde À La Fin Du Xixe Siècle, Lautréamont Et Mallarmé [M]. Paris: Éditions du Seuil, 1974. Revolution in Poetic Language. New York: Columbia University Press, 1984.

[60] Kristeva Julia. About Chinese Women [M]. London: Boyars, 1977.

[61] Lakoff and Johnsson, Metaphors we live by [M]. University of Chicago Press, 1980.

[62] Levi – Strauss Claude, Structural Antropology [M]. Translated by C. Jacobson and B. Schoepf. New York: Basic Books, 1963.

[63] Locke, John. An Essay Concerning Humane Understanding [M]. London: Thomas Bassett, 1690.

［64］ López – Varela, A. & Ananta Sukla (Eds.) The Ekphrastic Turn: Inter – Art Dialogues
［M］. New Directions in the Humanities book series. Champaign, University of Illinois Research Park, USA: Common Ground Publishing, 2015.

［65］ Lotman Yuri. On the semiosphere ［J］. Translated by Wilma Clark. Sign Systems Studies, 2005, 33 (1): 205 – 229.

［66］ Manetti G. Theories of the Sign in Classical Antiquity ［M］. Bloomington/Indianapo-
lis: Indiana University Press, 1993.

［67］ Morris Charles W. Signs, Language and Behavior ［M］. New York: Prentice –
Hall, 1946.

［68］ Nöth Winfried. Handbook of Semiotics ［M］. Indiana University Press, 1995.

［69］ Ockham William. Summa Logicae, i. 1317 – 1328 ［M］. Ed. Philotheus Boeh-
ner. New York: St. Bonaventure, 1951 – 1954.

［70］ Plato. Cratylus ［M］ //. c. 385BC. Trans. Benjamin Jowett. in The Collected Dialogues
of Plato Including the Letters. Ed. Edith Hamilton and Huntington Cairns. New York:
Pantheon Books Bollingen Series LXXI, 1961: 421 – 474.

［71］ Peirce Charles S. (1931 – 1958). Collected Papers, ed. C. Hartshorne and P. Weiss,
8 vols. Cambridge, Massachusetts: Harvard University Press; 1935; Vols. VII – VIII
ed. Arthur W. Burks Cambridge, MA: Harvard University Press, 1958.

［72］ Propp Vladimir. Morphology of the folktale ［M］. Austin: University of Texas
Press, 1968.

［73］ Robins Robert Henry. Ancient and mediaeval grammatical theory in Europe with particular reference to modern linguistic doctrine ［M］. London: Bell, 1951.

［74］ Saussure Ferdinand de. Course in General Linguistics ［M］. Trans. Wade
Baskin. London: Fontana/Collins, ［1916］ 1974.

［75］ Scotus Joannes Duns. Ordinatio, Liber Primus (Volume III) Opera Omnia, c.
1302 – 1303.

［76］ P. Carolus Balic. Rome: Typis Polyglottis Vaticanis ［M］. 1954.

［77］ Sebeok Thomas Albert. Is a Comparative Semiotics Possible? ［M］ //in Échanges et
Communications: Mélanges offerts á Claude Lévi – Strauss à l'occasion de son 60ème
anniversaire, ed. Jean Pouillon and Pierre Maranda. The Hague: Mouton, 1968,
614 – 627; reprinted in Sebeok, Contributions to the Doctrine of Signs. Lanham,
MD: University Press of America, 1985. 59 – 69.

［78］ Sebeok Thomas Albert. Semiotics: A Survey of the State of the Art ［M］ //Linguistics
and Adjacent Arts and Sciences, Vol. 12 of the Current Trends in Linguistics

series. Ed. T. A. Sebeok, The Hague: Mouton, 1974. 211 – 264; reprinted in Sebeok Contributions to the Doctrine of Signs. Lanham, MD: University Press of America, 1985: 1 – 45.

[79] Sebeok Thomas Albert. Neglected Figures in the History of Semiotic Inquiry: Jakob von Uexküll, 1979. Reprinted in Sebeok. The Sign & Its Masters [M]. Lanham, MD: University Press of America, 1989, 187 – 207.

[80] Sebeok Thomas Albert. Contributions to the Doctrine of Signs [M]. Lanham, MD: University Press of America, 1985.

[81] Sebeok Thomas Albert. The Sign & Its Masters [M]. Lanham, MD: University Press of America, 1989.

[82] Sextus Empiricus. Sextus Empiricus [M]. c. 200. Loeb Classical Library Edition. Trans. by R. G. Bury. London: Heinemann, 1917 – 1955.

[83] Shklovsky Viktor. Theory of Prose [M]. Trans. Benjamin Sher. Elmwood Park: Dalkey Archive, 1990.

[84] Todorov Tzvetan. Theories of the Symbol [M]. Trans. Catherine Porter, Ithaca: Cornell University Press, 1982 [1977].

[85] Vico, Giambattista. Scienza Nuova (Principi di Scienza Nuova d'intorno alla Comune Natura delle Nazioni) [M]. English translation from 1948 by Thomas Goddard Bergin and Max Harold Fisch, 1725. The Internet Archive: https: //archive. org/details/new-scienceofgiam030174mbp.

[86] Voloshinov Valentin. Marxism and the Philosophy of Language [M]. Trans. Ladislav Matejka and I. R. Titunik. Cambridge, Mass. : Harvard University Press, 1973 [1929].

[87] Wellek Renéand Austin Warren. Theory of Literature. (3rd) [M]. San Diego: Harcourt Brace Jovanovich, 1977.

[88] Yates Frances A. The art of Ramon Lull: An approach to it through Lull's theory of the elements [M]. Journal of the Warburg and Courtauld Institutes, 1954 (17): 115 – 173.

Chapter 2

Inter-semiotic Aspects of
Chinese Calligraphy

Chinese calligraphy is a special synthetic art form, incorporating both painting and literary aspects. The earliest calligraphical examples with some aesthetic effects appeared on the oracle bone scripts. The artistic elements of calligraphy manifested themselves through graphic structures caused by particular brush strokes. Calligraphy emerged as an artistic discipline in Han times, when there were about five alternative systems of graphic scripts available for drawing. Since the Wei and Chin dynasties, this half – painting – half – poem genre had been further developed in combination with the main schools of painting and accepted the same principle as the latter. Wang Xizhi (307 – 365) was called the sage of Chinese calligraphy, but its heyday came during the Tang period, when this art became a part of "state learning". In ancient China, every writer was also a calligraphist, and this art has survived to the present. Its aesthetic signifiers consist in the structure of the stroke lines within individual characters and their combinations in short texts, expressing proportional rhythm and inner drive at once. Although the contents of calligraphical works must be poetical, the literary part is in fact only secondary in its aesthetic function. As a formalist or abstract form of art, calligraphy had often been regarded as similar to and comparable with dance and music in terms of dynamic structure, for in all three arts, rhythmic movement is an element of the work. By replacing the brush with a knife and paper with stone, calligraphy is turned into the arts of signet and stone script, another popular genre.

Chinese characters retain pictographical elements in their structure. In semiotic terms, the graphical parts of characters can help arouse emotional, volitional and intellectual associations through the directly visual stimulus, thus producing rich denotations and connotations. In addition, the characters have multiple phonetical structures consisting of phoneme, sound and tones, producing a special musical dimension communication.

Moreover, because different characters share the same size, the shapes and forms of sequences of characters lead to rhythm and regularity in poetic texts, being suited to the arrangements of "duizhang" (matching of sounds and senses in a couple of sentences and reiterative locutions).

The history of Chinese calligraphy is as long as that of China itself. As the soul of fine arts, calligraphy maintains a close rapport with Chinese cultural development. This study aims to explore the iconic correspondences between Chinese calligraphy and their subject – matter, and develop their intermedial semiotic potential.

Generally, the traditional Chinese typology of writing is practical in character. The *Book of History* as the earliest compilation of official documents contains various types of writing, but its principle of classification is not concerned with rhetoric and functional problems. Instead, it tries to distinguish between the grades of relations of superiority and intimacy between addressers and addressees.

Later in the Han dynasty a new classification of writings covering 12 types appeared in *The History of the Han*: *Records of Literature and Arts*, and accepted the principle of uses and practical functions. The first literary typology appeared in *The Anthology of Zhao – Ming Prince* (in the Liang), in which the demarcation lines between the categories of literature, scholarship and documents were drawn up and the entire writing material was divided into 39 types accordingly. In the meantime the first book of Chinese criticism appeared, *Dragon Carvings of a Literary Mind*, presented a theory to further divide Chinese writing into 33 types.

Chinese uses Chinese characters known as *hanzi*. These are symbols, based on ancient iconic ideograms, and do not comprise an alphabet. This writing system, in which each character generally represents either a complete one – syllable word or a single – syllable part of a word, is called logo – syllabic. Each character has its own pronunciation. Being literate in Chinese requires memorizing about 4,000 characters.

Because many commonly used Chinese characters have 10 to 30 strokes, certain stroke orders have been recommended to ensure speed, accuracy and legibility in composition. So, when learning a character, one has to learn the order in which it is written, and the sequence has general rules, such as: top to bottom, left to right, horizontal before vertical, middle before sides, left – falling before right – falling, outside before inside, inside before enclosing strokes.

The strokes in Chinese characters fall into eight main categories: horizontal (一), vertical (|), left – falling (丿), right – falling (丶), rising (/), dot (丶), hook (亅) and turning (⌐, ㄴ, 乙, etc.). Correct stroke order, proper balance and rhythm of characters are all essential of Chinese calligraphy. The "Eight Principles of Yong" is an outline of how to write these strokes. They can all be found in the character for "yǒng" (永, which translates as "forever" or "permanence"). In many cases, a calligrapher will practice writing the Chinese character "永" many times in order to perfect the eight basic essential strokes contained within the letter. It was believed that the practice of these principles would ensure beauty in one's writing calligraphy.

Figure 2   Image of Chinese Character _Yong_ (永)

Source: < http: //en. wikipedia. org/wiki/Eight_ Principles_ of_ Yong >

The expression "Four treasures of the study" refers to the brush, ink, paper and ink stone used in Chinese and other East Asian calligraphic traditions. The head of the brush can be made of the hair (or feather) of a variety of animals, including wolf, rabbit, deer, chicken, duck, goat, pig and tiger, and sometimes even a newborn child, who would preserve this as a souvenir. The artist usually completes their work of calligraphy by adding their seal at the very end, in red ink. The seal serves as a signature and is usually done in an old style.

Many East Asian scripts (such as Chinese, Japanese and Korean) can be written horizontally or vertically, because they consist mainly of disconnected syllabic units, each conforming to an imaginary square frame. Traditional Chinese is written in vertical columns from top to bottom, the first columnis on the right side of the page, with the text starting on the right. In modern times, using a Western layout of horizontal rows running from left to right and being read from top to bottom has become more popular.

In Chinese calligraphy, Chinese characters can be written in five major styles. These styles are intrinsic to the history of Chinese script. The oldest style is "seal script" which continues to be widely practiced, although most people today cannot read it.

Figure 3   Image of Chinese Character *Zhuanshu* (篆) 書

Source: http://en. wikipedia. org/wiki/File: Seal_ Eg. png

In clerical script, characters are generally "flat" in appearance, and wider than in seal script and modern script, both of which tend to be taller than wider. Some versions of clerical are square and rectilinear.

Figure 4   Image of Chinese Character *Lishu*（隶書）

Source：http：//en. wikipedia. org/wiki/File：Clerical_ Eg. png

The semi – cursive script approximates normal handwriting, in which strokes and sometimes characters are allowed to run into one another. Here, the brush leaves the paper less often than with the regular script and characters appear less angular.

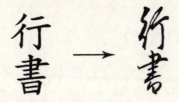

Figure 5   Image of Chinese Character *Xingshu*（行書）

Source：http：//en. wikipedia. org/wiki/File：Semi – Cur_ Eg. png

The cursive script is a fully cursive, with large simplifications and ligatures. It requires specialized knowledge to be read. Entire characters may be written without lifting the brush from the paper at all, and characters frequently flow into one another, being highly rounded and soft in appearance, with a noticeable lack of angular lines.

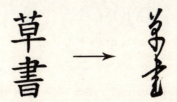

Figure 6   Image of Chinese Character *Caoshu*（草書）

Source：http：//en. wikipedia. org/wiki/File：Cur_ eg. svg

The regular script developed from a semi – cursive form of clerical script. As the name suggests, this script is "regular", with each stroke written slowly and carefully, the brush being lifted from the paper and all strokes distinct from each other.

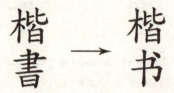

Figure 7   Image of Chinese Character *Kaishu* (楷書)

Source：http：//en. wikipedia. org/wiki/File：Regular_ Eg. png

In the ancient Chinese tradition, artists extracted the primary principle for artistic creation from real life: "Both ancient Chinese characters and mixed – seal characters are imitations of objects" (Suo Jing, 2007: 19 cited in Peng & Geng 127). WeiHeng (? – 291), a great Chinese calligrapher, argued that "Seal characters designed in the forms of birds and young frogs are pictographic scripts, which are created by imitating appearance of objects" (SuoJing, 2007: 14 cited in Peng & Geng, 127). With a history of over six thousand years, Chinese calligraphy, occurred initially in the New Stone Age, and then in the graphics sculptured in bronze during Shang and early Zhou Dynasty, the bird – pest calligraphy in the "Spring and Autumn Period", the seal script calligraphy in Qin and Han Dynasties, and the Song typeface in Song, Yuan, Ming and Qing Dynasties. All of these used materials as varied as bronze weapons, seals, pennant, bricks, tiles, paper-cut, cloth-embroidery, prints, and so on, a clear sign of its intermedial potential (Li Mingjun, 1996: 3) .

Furthermore, Marge Landsberg (1980) has noted that there are many languages, like Chinese, that contain elements which are not just symbolic and arbitrary. As mentioned in Charles S. Peirce's classification of signs, they also include iconic and imitative forms. According to Peirce (1839 – 1914), an icon is a non-arbitrary intentional sign, a designation which is to a significant degree representational and has some degree of isomorphism and resemblance to the object it designates. This paper draws attention to the iconic correspondences between Chinese calligraphy and their subject – matter in order to point out its intermedial qualities.

For Charles Sanders Peirce and the Harvard School of Pragmatism, a sign is an object standing for that an experience of the former affords knowledge of the latter in some respect or capacity. This includes sounds, images, gestures, scents, tastes, textures, words and so on. The sign creates in the mind a more developed sign, a mental effect or thought that Peirce calls "interpretant" and which gives the sign significance or meaning, becoming in turn a sign in a dynamic process ad infinitum. In Peirce's conception, signs can be divided into icons, indices and symbols. Symbols are arbitrary and unmotivated, reliant on conventional usage to determine meaning. Symbolic signs are agreed upon for given purposes and they can be found in most alphabets. Indices always point, reference, or suggest something else by means of Peirce outlined three types: tracks, symptoms, and designations. Tracks often have a physical, cause and effect relationship, but are not simultaneous with their object, i. e. foot or paw prints. Symptoms are simultaneous with their object, and distinguishing between symptom and object may be impossible, i. e. fever is a symptom of infection; smoke is a symptom of fire. Lastly, designations point or signify while being distinct from their object, i. e. proper names, a pointed finger, and the word "this". Finally, icons are signs that resemble what they stand for. Originally called "likenesses" by Peirce, icons have a "topological similarity" to their object, i. e. figurative painting—not surrealist or modern photographs. Peirce creates three subcategories of icon: image, metaphor and diagram. The relations of resemblance between "images" and objects are relatively simple, their attributes based on sensory qualities. Diagrams and their objects share structural relations even if they may have a degree of arbitrariness, i. e. maps and equations. Metaphors "represent the representative character of an object by representing a parallelism in something else" (Johansen, 2002: 40; also Burks "Icon, Index, and Symbol", 1949: 675). Though technically conveyed through the non – iconic symbols of language, this includes literary metaphors. Peirce's definition, however, remains much broader, with signs occupying several categories simultaneously, i. e. a thermometer is an index but also a metaphoric icon.

In Chinese artistic calligraphy, every character is a kind of creative decorative form designed by the artist who takes inspiration from nature. Chinese characters fall within six categories: self – explanatory characters, pictographs, picto – phonetic characters, associative compounds, mutually explanatory characters and phonetic loan characters. Among them, pictographs were used as the earliest form of writing and a basic way of words building, undoubtedly linked to drawing, and thus "describing objects as they are" (Xie He, 1997: 55, 479 – 502). Xu She also emphasized that hieroglyphic characters are learnt "from outside and made into words through painting" (Xu She, 2010: 4). Resemblance is an integral part of Chinese writing, no matter how simplified or abstracted. This fact conforms to Peirce's ideas where icons represent relations of direct imitation between signifier and signified on the basis of external peculiarities. (Peirce, 1885: 181) Thus, his theories have had a particular impact on the logic of imaging, graphic and intermedial signification (Michael Leja, "Peirce, Visuality, and Art", 2000: 26).

In Archaic Chinese Graphology, Jiang LiangFu claimed that:

> The overall spirit of the Chinese characters started with human life, or rather, from the entire body of human being's. The presence of all LIFE IS perceived by the senses of seeing, hearing, touching, smelling, tasting, and especially the sense of seeing is the most important. This has created the characters 牛, 羊, 虎 (ox, sheep, tiger) characterizing their heads. These parts are easily be recognized by people, and to create characters like 龙, 凤 (Chinese dragon, Chinese phoenix) which the luckiest signs and universally worshiped by Chinese (Jiang LiangFu, 1984: 66).

The characters like 日, 月, 水, 雨, 山 (sun, moon, water, rain and mountain) are also very typical examples of form imitation. By stylized drawings, they represent the appearance of the objects. 水 (shuǐ, "Water") represents the lines of a flowing river. 山 (shān, "Mountain") presents the undulating peaks of mountains. 爪 雨（yǔ, "Rain"）resembles the appearance of the rain coming from sky. The characte Ψ and Ϋ are easily recognized by imitating ox's and sheep's heads; while 𝔖（马, "horse"）ϸ（鸟, "bird"）and 𝔖（龟, "tortoise"）are the stylized drawings of the entire forms of their corresponding animals. The objects and their corresponding Chinese pictographic characters are shown in the following table.

Table 2   The Objects and Their Corresponding Chinese Pictographic Characters

objects	Regular Script（Simplified）	Pinyin	Meaning
☉	日	ri	Sun
𝔇	月	yuè	Moon
⛰	山	shān	Mountain
水	水	shuǐ	Water
雨	雨	yǔ	Rain
Ψ	牛	niú	Cow
Ϋ	羊	yáng	Goat
马	马	mǎ	Horse
ϸ	鸟	niǎo	Bird
龟	龟	guī	Tortoise

Source: http://en. wikipedia. org/wiki/Chinese_ character_ classification

There are also some types of calligraphy that are more imaginative. For example, Dragon's Claw Calligraphy, Tassel Calligraphy, Bird – pest Calligraphy or Tadpole Calligraphy, where additional imaginative details are added to the writing.

The origin of Tassel Calligraphy dates back to the mythology of Yan Emperor Shen – nung（神农）5000 years ago. Known as the Emperor of the Five Grains and the patron of agriculture in ancient China, Shen – nung taught ancient Chinese practices of agriculture and use of herbal drugs. After testing and tasting hundreds of plants, he finally discovered the tassel plant. He created one text for record and celebration, where the bottoms of character strokes look like tassels. Today, Chinese regard him and Yellow Emperor（XuanYuan Shi, 轩辕

氏）as father of the nation and branch ceremonies to worship every year. Shen - nung's tassel calligraphy created eight characters "日月盈晨、辰宿列张", which are so beautiful and elegant that they have become the wonders of world's writings. They reflect Shen- nung's great joy for the golden harvest.

Figure 8　Shen－nung's Tassel Calligraphy

Source：http：//blog. 163. com/shz6763814@ 126/blog/static/580934412010431105249685.

As another typical example, Tadpole Calligraphy is named for the strokes based on its appearance. It is written using a tadpole - like stroke with thick heads but thin tails. Tadpole calligraphy has been regarded as one of the eight original texts or symbols of China that are mysterious and would need further analysis.

Figure 9　Tadppole Calligraphy

Source：http：//baike. baidu. com/link? url = Qyiopdoy3o9qFsHHZX8UpGHE0mS66WL72aiCeXa － QcX 0lSVlR06FRGb － 2OogdgM8.

Bird – pest Calligraphy prevailed from the later Spring and Autumn Period to the Warring States Period in the south of ancient China. This calligraphy reflects vividly the ancient culture of these areas. The images of birds, insects and fish are added to the strokes and combined with Chinese characters. This kind of style often takes the form of golden gilding and looks noble and gorgeous. Hence, Bird – pest Calligraphy adorns many ancient Chinese weapons, containers and sacrificial vessels. The inscription on King Goujian's sword (King Goujian was King of Yue, famous for his perseverance in time of hardship) illustrates this point well. The attachment of images not only provides a decorative effect, but also adds to the complexity of the strokes, making the calligraphy unpredictable and quite difficult to identify. Therefore, sometimes Bird – pest Calligraphy was also used to inscribe flags to convey commands because it was difficult to decipher and falsify. After the Han dynasty this style was used primarily in seals and it evolved into a kind of art font.

Modern Chinese scholar, Guo Moruo (郭沫若, 1892 – 1978), commented that images of birds and pests were added to the calligraphy under aesthetic consciousness, and that it also emphasized their utility as decorative patterns on cloth. This was the origin of the first ancient Chinese references to calligraphy as arts work.

Figures 10 & 11   Flying White Calligraphy

Source: http: //baike. baidu. com/view/328118. htm.

With time, the strokes added to the characters in Chinese calligraphy incorporated the patterns taken from the natural world combined with abstractions. For example, a particular type of Chinese calligraphy known as Flying White Calligraphy came from cursive characters drawn with seals, and evolved into a novel style of calligraphy characterized by its hollow strokes done with a half – dry brush. Huang BoSi (1079 – 1118) who lived in Earlier Song Dynasty explained that "It takes that part same like silky hair to stand for white, cites its kinetic potential to fly as flying" (Huang Bosi. "Dongguan Yulun, Flying white", 2010: 83). Created by Cai Yong (133 – 192) in the Han Dynasty, the story tells that he was inspired by the artisans painting the walls of the Royal Library with a broom dipped in lime. This type of calligraphy came to be executed with bamboo rather than a brush. Because of the special brush technique applied, ribbon – like wide lines are left behind, giving an impression of jumping or leaping on the paper surface without losing contact with it, all executed in one stroke. Owing to this, Flying White becomes more of an aesthetic brush technique than a style, and it also has found favour in neighbouring countries, such as Japan. Kuukai (空海, 774 – 835) was a Buddhist monk, scholar and also possibly the greatest calligrapher of all time in Japan; in his work he brilliantly merged Flying White with semi – cursive script (行書).

Figure 12　Flying White with Semi – cursive Script

Source: http: //www. beyondcalligraphy. com/flying_ white_ script. html.

In the Tang dynasty of ancient China, symbolpainting was interwoven with Flying White, such as dragons, birds, or other motifs. The work of Empress

Wu (武则天, 624 – 705), the only empress in Chinese history, exemplified and illustrated this point well. She managed to develop her own style of Flying White decorated with bird drawings. Her work was like her character, strong, expressive and bold.

Figure 13   Image of Empress Wu's Flying White

Source: http: //www. beyondcalligraphy. com/flying_ white_ script. html.

Flower – Bird – Dragon – Phoenix Calligraphy (花鸟龙凤字) is also tremendously popular. It is a free cursive style with an auspicious and joyful meaning and a great visual appeal, where words and drawing are fused together. This kind of pictographic calligraphy originated during Han dynasty and thrived in Tang dynasty and now has become one of the popular categories of folk art in China. One of the reasons for its popularity is that a pictograph of a pair of Flower – Bird – Dragon – Phoenix can be finished very quickly, only in 3 to 5 minutes. The brushes for it are not ordinary ones and made from special materials. Once painted on the paper, it will appear as different colours. When observing an example, one is amazed by its interesting, vivid appearance and folk craftsmen's creativity. The patterns look like flowers, forests, ships or butterflies, but in fact the texts are people's names or encouraging phrases for wishes. Flower – Bird – Dragon – Phoenix Calligraphy incorporates characters and patterns effectively to show happiness and good luck. It embodies both traditional painting's clearness and western painting's colourfulness. Because of all these unique characteristics, Flower – Bird – Dragon – Phoenix Calligraphy lives up to its name as a rarity in China's history of culture.

Figure 14 家和万事兴, **meaning harmonious family makes everything prosperous**
Source: http://www. culture – sh. com/en/craft/CraftItem. aspx? ID = 11.

Chinese characters evolve from pictures and signs, and the art ofcalligraphy develop naturally from this special writing system. The Ancient Chinese use calligraphy to communicate by using strokes companied with painting to pursue the beauty of nature and man's spirit. Luxun（鲁迅, 1881 – 1936）said that calligraphy is painting. Chinese calligraphy maintains the beauty factor in nature and has exactly the same origin as painting.

Eave tiles use characters, suns, moons, and stars; Graph – Text uses carriages and horses; Floral Currency employs turtles and cranes; Jia Qing porcelain shows characters organized by pines, and so on. Eave tiles are small accessories in classical Chinese architecture fixed at the end of rafters for decoration and for shielding the eaves from wind and rain. They emerged as a culture in their own light during the Zhou Dynasty（c. 11th century – 771 B. C.）and reached their zenith during the Qin and Han Dynasty（221 B. C. – 220 A. D.）. In the inter-ring years, Eave tiles underwent the transition from a half – round design to a cy-lindrical design, and from plain surface to decorative patterns, from intaglio to bas – relief carvings, from lifelike imagery to abstraction, and from patterns to inscriptions, until they became an art that involved many intermedial aspects, including language, literature, aesthetics, calligraphy, carving, decoration and architecture, with themes that ran the gamut from nature and ecology to mythology, totems, history, palaces, yamens, mausoleums, place names, auspicious phrases, folklore, and family names. Together the eaves tiles form a history book that reflects vividly the natural scenery, humanities, political science and economics.

Figure 15　Images of Eaves Tiles with Chinese Calligraphy

Source：http：//www. chinaculture. org/classics/2008-05/06/content_ 132864_ 2. htm.

　　In addition, some calligraphy styles scenes are taken from popular myths, folklore, and historical figures. The iconicity of these themes is always fused with the creator's ideographic thinking, for instance Monk Tang's "Pilgrimage to the West".

　　Based on the changeable shape of Chinese characters, Shenzhi Poetry (神智诗) was formed in ancient China and characteristic of its witty literary style. These poems would not be written directly on paper, but expressed by poets through presenting characters' abnormal formation appearance, including the size, thickness, length, order density, the amount of strokes, missing strokes, the height etc methods. People need to read these poems not only as a visual experience but also in their guessing ability, like playing word games. Only in this way, readers can comprehend the ingenious design of the poems and the hidden wisdom of poets. Su Shi, a literary figure from the Song Dynasty, was believed to be the creator of this kind of poetry. His works are regarded as the most classical Shenzhi examples of poetry in ancient Chinese calligraphy history.

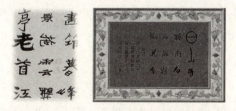

Figures 16 & 17　Images of Shenzhi Poetry

长亭短景无人画，老大横拖瘦竹筇。回首断云斜日暮，曲江倒蘸侧山峰。

——《晚眺》苏轼

一山路邡雨袅舟燃过风花香

In Chinese thought, the secular and the sacred are contemplated as opposites interlinked in harmonious proportions. While the secular world is reflected in the liveliness of natural depictions, the sense of holiness and timelessness also permeates these images. Much of the sacred timelessness is inspired in Zen (Chán meaning "absorption" or "meditation"), a school of Mahayana Buddhism that originated in China during the 6th – century. Traditionally, the origin of Chán in China is credited to the monk Bodhidharma, recorded as having come from India during the time of Southern and Northern Dynasties. The idea that the ultimate reality is present in the daily world of relative reality fitted into Chinese culture, which emphasized the mundane world and society.

Seng Zhao's *Zhaolun* (*Treatises of Seng zhao*) is perhaps the most significant text for the study of the early Mādhyamika School (549 – 623 CE), a philoso-phical development that arose within Mahāyāna Buddhism in India during the f irst few centuries CE, and its relationship to the indigenous Daoist and Confucian traditions. As Qingben Li (2013) points out, Mahāyāna concentrates on showing how signs, representing concepts and ideas as well as real objects, should not be contemplated with a false sense of duality between subject and object.

It is like a man pointing a finger at the moon to show it to others who should follow the direction of the finger to look at the moon. If they look at the finger and mistake it for the moon, they lose (sight of) both the moon and the finger. Why? Because the bright moon is actually pointed at; they both lose sight of the finger and fail to distinguish between (the states of) brightness and darkness. In doing so, they mistake the finger for the bright moon and are not clear about brightness and darkness. (Qingben Li, 2013: 38)

Seng Zhao (僧肇 384 –414) recognized the significance of movement and stillness in giving birth to Yin and Yang. Movement contributes to separation, while stillness engenders combination. Self – awareness in Zen results from the alternation of these two principles: "It is necessary to find stillness in the movement of things because, despite their movement, things reside in a constant state of stillness (Seng Zhao, 1999, cited in Qingben Li, 39) . " Seng Zhao understood nature as a motion that never ends, beneath whose surface lies stillness. He explains that past events only exist in the past, and present things only exist in the present, so there is no connection between past and present and hence no change or movement. The word "harmony" came to signify "without conflict" from around the time of Lao Zi (571 – 471BC). This harmony is embodied in the abstract symbol "He", which means "and" in Chinese, coming to describe the unity of non – identical things (Zhang Dainian, *Key Concepts in Chinese Philosophy*, 2005: 270)

The metaphor of a celestial wheel is used by Zhuang Zhou (369 – 286 BC) to explain how "all things belong to their own species, their births and deaths coming again and again manifested in different situations. The beginning and the end of this alternate progress is just like a great wheel rotating without stop. Nobody is able to find the sequence in which things have happened" (Zhuang zhou, 2009: 171). This view is present in Tao, "the connection between Yin and Yang" (Confucius, 2010: 290), an "opening and closing named 'change'" (Confucius, 2010: 298). Yang is the power of creation, while Yin nourishes life. Both interact and produce innumerable variations, seasonal patterns, plant renewing, fading, decay and death, new birth, etc. Owning to this central idea, Chinese calligraphy is articulated in an intermedial harmonious equilibrium that puts together the popular and the divine, as well as sound and image, writing and painting.

For example, the popular decorative character 寿 shou (longevity) is used to express abundance of blessings, and visually the amount of strokes conveys this idea, while the stretching and undulating forms transmit the meaning of immortality. 寿 is sometimes drawn in a composition with ancient coins in order to convey the progress of longevity. In ancient Chinese culture, coins also are named for 泉（quan）which sounds like 全（quan, meaning together/ full-ness）. The Chinese pronunciation of a bat sounds 蝙蝠（bianfu）; while the pronunciation of the character 蝠 is identical to the character 福（fu, meaning happiness）. The following picture（Figure 1）with images of the bat, the ancient coin and the character 寿, conveys good wishes and a deep meaning that happiness and longevity will last forever. The plant presented in the picture is Ganoderma lingzi（灵芝）, regarded as fairy plant and a symbol of happiness in ancient China.

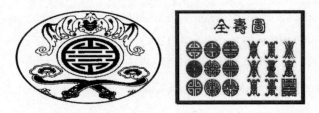

Figures 18 & 19   Images of Chinese Character *Shou*

Source：http：//image. baidu. com/i? tn = baiduimage&ipn = r&ct = 201326592&cl = 2&fm = index&lm = − 1&st = − 1&sf = 2&fmq = &pv = &ic = 0&nc = 1&z = &fb = 0&istype = 2&ie = utf − 8&word = % E5% AF% BF% E5% AD%97% E5%9B% BE% E7% 89% 87&f = 3&oq = % E5% AF% BF% E5% AD%97% E5%9B% BE&rsp = 0.

Besides, the creation of Chinese character Biáng also can serve as a good example. Premier Li Si in the Qin Dynasty is traditionally credited with the invention of the Biáng character, but in a popular version, it was a poor scholar in Xian city who, inspired by the sound of dough being drummed "Biang Biang", created the character. "Biang" is a complex character made of 58 strokes of various types. Xian and Shanxi providence residents describe the graphic patterns in "Biang" using the following visual song：

> A point rises up to heaven, and the yellow river has two bends. The character "eight"（八）opens its mouth, and the character "speak"（言）walks in. You make a twist, I make a twist,（幺 "tiny"）you grow, I grow（長）, and we add a horse（馬）king in between. The character "heart"（心）forms the base, the character "moon"（月）stands at the side, a hook（刂 "knife"）at the right to hang sesame candies, and we ride a carriage to tour（radical：辶 "walk"）the streets of Xianyang.

Figure 20   Image of Chinese Charater *Biáng* (邉)

Source: http: //en. wikipedia. org/wiki/File: Bi% C3% A1ng_ % 28regular_ script%29. svg.

"Biang" conveys the idea of simultaneity, being here and there, present and past, earthly and heavenly, popular and sacred. But it also conveys the intermedial multiplicity of Chinese calligraphy. "Biang" is sound, image, and cultural metaphor at the same time.

The Chinese character feng (the wind) is created when a pictograph foran-insect [chong, originally hui, a type of snake (Figure 1)], is placed inside the character fan, which means the origin (Figure 2). The resulting character (Figure 3) is explained in an ancient Chinese text as: "when the wind blows, insects are born. " This meaning of feng has evolved due a multitude of cultural influences and beliefs, the belief that wind "lives" in caves before rushes out into the world, that all kinds of insects live in caves, that both wind and insects are a cause of destruction for man. These all led to the "when the wind blows, insects are born" interpretation. The wind is also viewed as a "pernicious influence", that windy weather can cause disease, again a perciveved distructive force. The simplified version (Figure 4) keeps the meaning of movement of the air in the Eastern and Western cultures. (Subhuti Dharmananda, http: //www. itmonline. org/articles/feng/feng. htm)

Another type of folk calligraphy is a palindrome, which conveys the principles of non – duality and Zen, offering the visual metaphor of a cyclic and dynamic view of space – time.

Chong or Hui Fan   Feng   Feng   raditional version   simplified version

A palin dromemay be written in different forms, either as short couplet or a traditional poem, it is a word, phrase, number or other sequence of units that has the property being read in either direction. A Chinese word is not composed of letters or syllables, but a character. Chinese palindromes have to be phrases or sentences and are much easier to construct than in languages written with an alphabet. The adjustment of punctuation and spaces between words is generally permitted (for several examples see Peng and Geng, 2013).

"可以清心""以清心可""清心可以""心可以清"

May make a heart pure, being pure make a heart, a pure heart can be permitted, a heart can be made pure

"月是故乡明""是故乡明月""故乡明月是""乡明月是故""明月是故乡"

The moon is bright in hometown; is the hometown bright moon; the hometown bright moon is it; hometown is bright for the moon; the bright moon is hometown.

Su Hui (苏蕙, 357 - ?) was a Chinese poet from the Pre - Qing period. She was well known for renovating the genre and producing the most visually and structurally impressive palindrome masterpiece to date. Using multi-colored silks, she wove the poem onto brocade. Her poem consists of 841 characters and is in the form of a twenty - nine by twenty - nine character grid. This example can be read in any directions, forward, backwards, vertically, horizontally, diagonally. It may even be read within its color - coded grids. Su Hui's works is regarded as one of miracles of Chinese literary history.

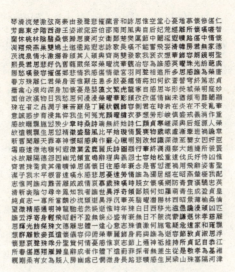

Figure 21   Images of Pallindrome

Source : http : //image. baidu. com/.

Some Chinese expressions employ metaphorical images to convey meaning. For instance, the expression of love can take the form of two butterflies, two swallows, fish or lotus.

Figure 22   Images of Love

Source: http: //image. baidu. com/i? tn = baiduimage&ipn = r&ct = 201326592&cl = 2&lm = -.

Liu Xie (465 – 520) explained that the feelings hide beyond words and that forms only partially show their meaning (2007: 226), with much meaning remaining "hidden" in "empty spaces" through which the readers would be able to create interpretations based on their own feelings, thoughts OR experiences, as in Qingben Li (2013) shows in the example of Wáng Wéi's poem "Dwelling in

Mountain and Autumn Twilight". This means that Chinese characters embody a dynamic quality which is much related to Zen principles. Finally, the Tao symbol of Yin and Yang itself represents heaven as a circle and earth as a square (a sphere and a cube in tri – dimensional representation):

> Utmost Yang is solemn, somber; utmost Yin is brilliant, shinning. The solemn and somber comes from heaven; the brilliant and shinning comes from earth. The two intermingle, interpenetrate, perfect harmony and so things are generated from them. (Confucius, 2010: 314)

When Yin and Yang are connected to spirit and matter, ideas and their representations (signs); reunited creation takes place; separated death occurs. As shown, Chinese calligraphy captures this complex dynamics and correlation between the visual, the sonic, reality and imagination.

The culture of the ancient Chinese calligraphy texts, also gives new charm in the modern life. The official logo and pictograms designed for Beijing Olympic Games can serve as perfect examples to this. The inspiration for creating these pictograms originates mainly from Chinese characters. The logo for Beijing Olympic Games entitled "Dancing Beijing" features a stylized calligraphic character 京 (jīng, means capital) thus referring to the host city.

As for pictograms, in ancient China they were made of strokes of seal characters as basic forms and integrated the pictographic charm of inscriptions on bones and bronze objects, becoming the simplified embodiment of modern graphics. The pictograms for Beijing Olympics are praised as the beauty of seal characters. They showcase the appealing and flowing beauty of seal characters fully. For instance, the pictogram for swimming is made up of two parts. The top element is the brief symbol for a person; the bottom element is the symbol for water. Seve-ral curved strokes are applied to express the flowing of water in the pictogram for swimming. Another example is from the pictograms for athletics and football. Both of them originate from the seal character (舞) in order to show the visual effect of running actions. By using lines, these two pictograms not only express the attractiveness of sport spirit but also are aesthetically pleasing The pictograms for Beijing Olympics illustrate well the effects of sharp contrast between the black and white colours, just as used in the traditional Chinese artistic form of rubbings.

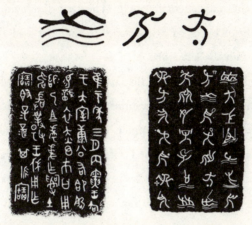

Figures 23 & 24   Images of Chinese Rubbing Form and Pictograms for Beijing Olympics
Source: http://creativerepository.com/2010/01/14/evolution – of – olympic – pictograms – 1964 – to – 2012/.

The pictograms of the Beijing Olympics display a distinct character of motion, a graceful aesthetic perception of movement and rich cultural connotations, thus arriving at the harmony and unity of form with conception.

To conclude, Chinese characters are complex signs that rely on hybrid combinations of different types of signs, as distinguished by Harvard pragmatist Charles S. Peirce. The paper has shown the intermedial qualities of Chinese calligraphy and the influence of Zen Buddhism upon traditional Chinese writing in general. Signs are shown as complex structures that mediate between reality and human interpretation, tinted with cultural and ideological significances.

Calligraphy, Confucianism and Taoism

Chinese calligraphy enjoyed the influence of various thought sources. The last part of this paper deals with the influence of Confucianism and Taoism upon

Chinese calligraphy. It explores the possibility of the dialogue and transformation between the traditional calligraphic theory and modern aesthetics of calligraphy. There are two aspects to be considered. One is the influence of philosophy on a certain calligraphic creation. The other is the study of the relationship between philosophical thought and calligraphy itself. The first deals with a particular style and variability. The ecocnd with invariance, aesthetics and theory. I will be mostly concerned with the latter one.

As seen in this chapter, each calligraphic style has special features that involve the use of the brush, the application of inks and shi – making. In China, all these tasks were performed by statemen—scholars who contemplated calligraphy as part of their political and moral role. According to traditional Tao and Confucian doctrines, philosophy and art was part of the cultural apparatus of the state to ensure the good relation between nature and humanity, and make sure skills were cultivated to preserve morality and ethics. Thus, all the elements, the use of ink, the tracing of the Chinese characters, and the use of the brush, are intended towards the same objective.

The use of ink enjoyed a certain degree of independence. Liu Xicai, a scholar in the Qing dynasty, explained that the ink was like the veinswhile the brust was the substance inside which directes the performance. In turn, the character is the shape that becomes communicable by the action of the brush, driven by the calligrapher's mental expression. The shape of the character is not just a communicative semantic expression. It also expresses the calligrapher's desires, intention and temperament in the way it may be tilted, elongated, and so on. The calligrapher's inner energy shi drives the shape into a dynamic form which is not pre – fixed but exists in its variability and probability of being.

In Western semiotics, writing is a process that fixes the letters in the alphabetic system, and where sound and its graphic materiality (signifier) contain the concept arising in the speaker's mind and written representation (signified). This concept refers to something that exists in the external world. According to Saussure, the relationship between the signifier and the signified is arbitrary, estab-

lished by usage. On the other hand, Chinese characters, the relationship contained between the symbol or character – shape and the concept is based on appearance; on similarity with the object it denotes. It is more an icon or figure
than an abstract symbol based on an arbitrary association with sound. The form of
writing and the sound are unified in the character shape with the signified image.
For this reason, there are so many dialectal variations in China, with great pronunciation gaps. In short, in Chinese, the character shape and the meaning are
uniformed in writing, but the sound and meaning are separate in pronunciation.
They capture and fix the image of things, not the sound. The development sequence is from charaeter shape to meaning, then from character – shape – meaning to sound. In Western languages, pronunciation, spelling, and meaning are
built into one body. The pronunciation decides the spelling and the spelling ref
lects the pronunciation. In Chinese, the pronunciation may diller greatly, but
the character is always uniformed and does not reflect pronunciation by nature.

　　Thus, in Chinese calligraphy, the character-shape functions uniting the by-
gone perceptual experience of things (objects and people) in the outside world,
with the calligrapher operating as a mediator in the unification. His exis-ting state
as an specific individual, his style—which reveals his interior state-originate from
his own spirit, based on his phenomenological apprehension, without laws or
regulations. Therefore, each calligraphic works is considered unique and cannot
be copied. When we face a calligraphic workm, it is tacit understanding that
leads us to discern the *Shi* (the style of the character-shape).

　　While in the West and in Chinese printing, the emphasis is placed on communicability and usefulness under the governance of shared laws that establish certain kinds of semiotic relationships in order to achieve objectivity and universality,
in Chinese calligraphy there is not such "functional" use of significance. The
feelings of the calligrapher participate in the communicative situation and are not
alienated and instrumentalized for the sake of objectivity. Existence appears in its
limited, unknowable, ambiguous states of being. The character – shapes are not
controllable, evident and realistic. Thet are not limited by the world of fact.

They exist as an ideal that comes into being in the strangeness and the originality of writing, encompassing thought and mood. The calligrapher listens to his own interior self while perceiving the world of facts. His contemplation and attention helps fix in each trace and shape an intentionality that is not instrumental and can not be replicated.

Each unique character comes into being through the ink applied. The brush represents the action, the activity of non – regulated writing. Each type of brush (soft, hard and mixed) performs a different purpose according to the mental frame of mind of the calligrapher. The performance of the brush yield the character – shapes and the intention of the calligrapher's heart and mind. The materiality of the brush, the medium, is a state of nothingness, of self – negation, until it is penetrated by the calligrapher's intentionality. The brush shows the traces of ancient Chinese wisdom: let material be void to let the spirit appear. Therefore calligraphy is an art of spirinlal apprehending instead of perceptual appreciation. It is superior over traditional Chinese painting in this way.

In ancient Chinese painting, the truth it emphasized is not the natural truth seen by vision. But rather the natural truth intuited or penetrated only by soul. Nature in the former is considered *substance* that can be measured and studied by a given system of knowledge (logic, empirical science etc.). In calligraphy, the process is sing as a dynamic evolving system between Yang and Ying, two kinds of physical universal energy. While in the West, nature is dealt with and mainly viewed as substance containing laws and determined by a first principle of origin (creator, motor etc.), in China, Tao means a dynamic nothingness that remains possibility to be done, and nature is a process, not a substance. This emptiness of substance means that Chinese philosophy seems to lack the expression of a method. Indeed, it is rather a non – method of intentionality of non – sense. The aim of calligraphy lies in the use of this nothingness to create a sensous form. The technique involved creates from interior to exterior, and not the reverse, as it occurs in Western representation. In the history Chinese calligraphy, the emergence at every new calligraphic styie was fumdamentally bred in the personality and self-cultivation. The difference in the variaus personalities resulted in the various calligraphic styles described in this chapter. The most important are those by Yan Zhenqing and Liu Gangquan during the Tang Dynasty, and Su Dongpuo in the Song Dynasty. Mental effort and temperament inspired these artists, and their spirit materialized in their brush, causing the *Shi* come into form in the character that is between existence and nihility.

REFERENCES

［1］ Burks Arthur W. Icon, Index, and Symbol ［J］ Philosophy and Phenomenological Research, 1949 (9).

［2］ Confucius (孔子). Xici xia (系辞下) ZhouYi (周易). Trans. Guo Yu (郭彧). Beijing：Zhonghua book company, 2010.

［3］ Confucian Analects, Yang Huo. Trans. James Legge. The Four Books ［M］. Hu Nan PubJishing House, 1996.

［4］ Huang Bosi (黄伯思). Dongguan Yulun, "Flying white" (东观余论) ［M］//Selected Writings of Previous Dynasties' Calligraphy (历代书法论文选续编). Shanghai：Shanghai Calligraphy and Painting Press, 2010.

［5］ Jiang LiangFu (姜亮夫). Archaic Chinese Graphology (古文字学) ［M］. Hang Zhou：The People Press of Zhejiang, 1984.

［6］ Johansen Jorgen Dines. Signs in Use：An Introduction to Semiotics ［M］. New York：Routledge, 2002.

［7］ Landsberg Marge E. The Icon in Semiotic Theory ［J］. Current Anthropology, 1980 (21).

［8］ Lao Tsu Tao Te Ching, One, Trans. Gia-Fu-Feng and Jane English, Vintage Books, New York：A division of Rardom House, 1972.

［9］ Liu Xiz. Principle of an (Chinese version), trans. Song Xiangrui, Shanghai Ancient Books Publishing House, 1964.

［10］ Li Qingben (李庆本). Intersemiotic Translation：Zen and Somaesthetics in Wáng Wéi's poem "Dwelling in Mountain and Autumn Twilight" ［J］ Vishvanatha Kaviraja Institute, Orissa, India, Journal of Comparative Literature and Aesthetics, 2013

(36): 37 - 46.

[11] Li Mingjun（李明君）. An Illustrated history of Artistic Calligraphy in China（中国美术字图史说）. [M] Beijing: The People and Art Press, 1996.

[12] LiuXie（刘勰）. Being hidden and shown（隐秀）. The Outline of Chinese Aesthetic History（中国美学史大纲）[M]. Ye Lang（叶朗）. Shanghai: The People Press of Shanghai, 2007.

[13] Liu Rong. Amazing Chinese EavesTiles. http://www. chinaculture. org/classics/2008 - 05/06/content_ 132864_ 2. htm.

[14] Luk Charles. The Surangama Sutra [M]. Buddha Dharma Education Association Inc.

[15] Peirce Charles Sanders. On the Algebra of Logic: A Contribution to the Philosophy of Notation [J]. American Journal of Mathematics, Johns Hopkins University Press, 1885 (7).

[16] Peirce Charles Sanders. Peirce on Signs. Writings on Semiotics [M]. Chapel Hill: University of North Carolina Press, 1991.

[17] Peirce（皮尔斯）, Logic as Semiotic: The Theory of Signs（作为指号学的逻辑: 指号论）[M] // Selected Writings of Charles Sanders Peirce（皮尔斯文选）. Trans. Tu Jiliang（涂纪亮）. Beijing: Social Sciences Academic Press, 2006.

[18] Peng Lingling Yang Geng: Cultural Semiosis in Artistic Chinese Calligraphy [J] Cultura. International Journal of Philosophy of Culture and Axiology , 2013 (10): 127 - 140.

[19] Seng Zhao. Zhao lun（肇论）, Great Treatise on the Perfection of Wisdom（大智园正圣僧肇法师论）, Classic essence in Zen（禅宗经典精华）（Vol. 1）Beijing: Religious culture Press, 1999.

[20] SuoJing（索靖）. The Tendency Of Cursive（草书势）[M] //Selected Writings of Previous Dynasties' Calligraphy（历代书法论文选）. Shanghai: Shanghai Calligraphy and Painting Press, 2010.

[21] Subhuti Dharmananda. FENG: The Meaning of Wind in Chinese Medicine with special attention to acupoint fengchi（GB – 20）.

[22] http://www. itmonline. org/articles/feng/feng. htm. WeiHeng（卫恒）. Siti Shushi（四体书势）. Selected Writings of Previous Dynasties' Calligraphy（历代书法论文选）. Shanghai: Shanghai Calligraphy and Painting Press, 2010.

[23] Xie He（谢赫）. Explanations of Ancient Paintings（古画品录）[M]. Shanghai

Chinese Classics Publishing House, 1991.

[24] Xu She (许慎). Shuo Wen Jie Zi Xu (说文解字序) [M] // Selected Writings of Previous Dynasties' Calligraphy (历代书法论文选续编). Shanghai: Shanghai Calligraphy and Painting Press, 2010.

[25] Zhang Dainian. Key Concepts in Chinese Philosophy [M]. Beijing: Foreign Languages Press, 2005.

[26] Zhuang Zhou (庄周). Zhuang Zi (庄子) [M]. Beijing: Public Literature and Art Press, 2009.

Chapter 3

Multidimensional Cross-cultural Semiotics

Culture is about the transmission of both information and communication, including messages that carry not just conscious knowledge but also unconscious and emotional content, such as values, ethical and religious views, aesthetic imprint (what is good or bad related to what is beautiful or ugly), and so on.

It is important to distinguish between information and communication, although in practice this is not easy. Information theory was mostly developed in the 20th – century by North – American telecommunications engineer Claude Shannon (1916 – 2001). In Shannon's view, information is simply data received by machines, but also humans. Data is coded in mathematical algorithms and contained in signals. The decoding of signals in artificial languages uses different cognitive operations to the decoding of signs, part of human natural languages. Shannon devised this model in order to improve the efficiency of telecommunication systems (he was working for the Bell Company which, for example, developed the first analogic telephone) showed that the information contained in a signal is inversely proportional to its probability. In other words, that an ordered series of data such as 1, 2, 3, 4, 5 carries less information than a disordered one, like 2, 34, 58, 1050, 157. This is so because in the first series, the probability of 6 following 5 is very high, whereas in the second series any number can follow 157, so the probable information behind it is much higher. Shannon also introduce the concept of noise which refers to interfering elements in the channel (the physical system that carries the transmitted signal, it can be biologi-cal, like vocally produced sound waves or electronic). Shannon showed that e-ven if noise is present in the channel (in the form of electronic charge, or inter-fering exterior sound) the message can be decoded. Furthermore, noise can be-come part of the message, adding unexpected elements to it. However, Shannon's model, based on formal artificial languages (mathematical) for ma-chine communication does not provide information about the meanings in the natural languages used for human communication.

This discussion is relevant in the context of digital culture. As we shall see in the last chapter of this research, digital culture makes use of several layers of lan-guages, thus having complex semiotics. Some layers are natural language; others a formal mathematical codes (such as binary code made up of 1 and 0 to indicate the passing of electricity or not). Binary code is the most basic formal (also called artificial) language in computers. But there other layers of artificial languages un-til we get to the superficial surface, also called "interface", which uses human na-tural language, that is, analogic and non－digital. Analogic means that the signs that form it resemble, in some way, perceived reality. The most common ones are "images" (which may include pictures, photographs, graphs, maps, and also moving pictures as in cinema).

Contemporary culture is made up of all these signs: analogic and digital. More and more digital machines (computers, laptops, cell-phones) are com-bined with analogic forms of representation. For instance, when we visit a mu-seum, we can use our cell－phone to connect and acquire additional information about the building.

Cultural exchanges of information and communication within a given com-munity contribute to create a sense of connectness among members. This is what we call "identity". In the age of Globalization, cultural identity is a pointed and hotly debated question in academia. Cultural identity involves a core of traditional values and the recognition of several developing layers: the individual, the com-munity and the nation. The traditional essentialist view of identity derived from biological ties and a shared cultural core that involved a common language, similar customs, shared values and religion, aesthetic taste and so on. More recently, the constructivist perspective holds that identity is malleable and fluid, a socio – cultural construct that depends of certain dominant discourses in the community. These discourses also give shape to individual identities as a result of the semiotic interactions that take place in the social environment to which the individual belongs. Identity is then a process, a dialectical construction between various systems, the community's dominant field of reference (nation, region, city) , the social group to which the individual belong (family, friends, educational institutions, work environment, and so on) , and his or her subjective preferences.

Thus, the cross – cultural paradigm we propose here is based upon constructionist tenets, and contemplates several levels of syntagmatic and paradigmatic analysis and interpretative scales within culture. The studies to be presented in the following pages offer successive re – interpretations and translations, in the wide sense of the word, that show the complex multidimensional patterns present in culture, and that suggest that global identity is the result of a dialogue between territories; a dialogue performed by means of semiotic interchanges present in cultural products that were exchanged across nations. We shall focus on a range of these cultural products; including texts, images, firm and theatre, as well as contemporary forms of digital culture.

The constructionist model for multidimensional cross – cultural studies results from a semiotic understanding of interpretation as negotiation In other words, it puts contextual (spatiotemporal) communication at its core, including the interpretative system and its correlation with the object sought. This view no longer contemplates de concept of reality as pure objectivity, but a plurality of possible realities that can be brought to a consensual set of results – consequences by communicative intervention. Plausibility becomes more appropriate to describe the nature of scientific laws, without departing completely from what is actually experience or observed directly. It is ananti – essentialist and critical understanding of the access to knowledge, which is contemplated as a construction we use to interpret the real, dependent on daily semiotic interactions between individuals and their communities.

In our understanding, language is not simply a way of expression, but a form of action. Understanding of the world comes not just from our experienced reality, but from other people's understanding, through education, the advice we receive, the things we see others do, and also from the past, by means of recorded forms of information (books, videos, and so on). In multicultural communities, common so cio – cultural realities are constructed from interpretative conflicts that usually happen at a local level. Border zones have always had cross – cultural patterns that gave them a particularly fluid identity. In today's hyper – connected world, the sharing of stories across the World Wide Web creates the climate for ever increasing points of cultural contact. One of our arguments is that the emotional content of art makes the stories it may transmit more easily understood by others because dialogue and negotiation is always more successful when we learn to understand not just the reasons and motives behinds other people's actions, but also when we learn to put ourselves in their position by means of empathy.

Indeed, appreciation is an important aspect that works towards social construction since abstract theories are normative and though the may have the potential to influence social order, this would depend on whether or not people accept it, reject it or are indifferent to it. Appreciation also stems from a sense of trust towards the other, and has a generative capacity to challenge guiding dominant cultural assumptions in order to reconsider the apparently self – evident, and provide new alternatives for social action (guided by prescribed ideas, beliefs, intentions, and so on). Cross – cultural transformation is achieved when human behavior changes these conventional patterns that have a strong effect on the nature of social reality. The most powerful vehicle that communities have to convert agreements or arrangements in norms, values, goals, ideology is the act of dialogue. Therefore, the changes taking place in semiotic practices (the exchange of diverse forms of signs) can cause profound changes in social practices.

The multidimensional cross – cultural paradigm engages with the study of art because of its appreciative potential. As each community creates a set of stories that come together in what is called local culture, the reading and adaptation (to other formats) of these stories and of the latent emotional content within them increase the potential for others to assess and valorize these personal meanings, creating a positive link with the experiences of a given community. The heroes of those stories are remarkable people who represent the community's potential for future success. From an anthropological perspective, the myths and stories that conform the cultural heritage of a community have the potential to engage other communities in understanding their experiences, their values and their beliefs.

In the concrete case of contemporary China, two dominant cultural tendencies can be seen: conservatism and protectionism. This has resulted in rejecting Western discourse to preserve a supposedly unchangeable Chinese identity. Comparative models that study cultural and literary exchanges between China and the West were based on dualist perceptions of spatiotemporal orientation. The multi – dimensional model of cross – cultural research espoused in this research re – examines the relationships between Chinese and Western cultures. It also examines the misappropriation, transplantation, transfer and transformation of cultural representations and theories across diverse historical periods.

As opposed to the dualist model of traditional comparators approaches, where relations are simplified to A influences B. The multi – dimensional model operates complex mapping, between ancient Chinese culture and Western culture, and then back to modern Chinese culture. An example is offered in the following chapter in order to show the complexity of cross – cultural exchanges over time. Thus, chapter seven will focus on Ji Junxiang's *The Orphan of Zhao*, its sources, (mis) adaptations and critical interpretations, while the present chapter remains mainly theoretical in scope.

Viewed as diachronic processes, Modernization and Globalization have been interpretively derived from the concept of Westernization in the eyes of many scholars, both Eastern and Western. In the postcolonial milieu, Edward Said marked "Orientalism" a product of Western culture and a projection of Western subjectivity and power (Said, 1979: 12). As Liu Kang and Jin Hengshan argue in "Post – colonial Criticism: from the West to China" (1998), much postcolonial criticism, while grounded in the Orient, are not real oriental discourse given the multicultural multiethnic background of scholars who, like Said, formulate them. Their academic upbringing is still clearly positioned in the West, signaling the location of knowledge in Western publishing houses.

Once defined as "a pattern of thinking and behavior manifested through the activities of a nation (...) that distinguishes it from other nations" (Benedict, 1988: 45 – 46), nations are no longer mono – cultural. Among the "Effects of Globalization on Literary Study" (1997), J. Hillis Miller noted the impact of new technologies and modes of production and consumption, as well as the socio – cultural re – organization of local communities as well as nation states.

The awareness of the importance of cultural policies for nation consolidation led first to protective and conservative positions in many countries, promoting local knowledge production and preserving the idea of national identity and culture. During the 1990s, many countries, including China, were concerned about the possibility of losing one's traditional culture with the influx of cultural products particularly addressed to the younger generations (television, music, the Internet). Protective efforts came to reject all influence from the outside world.

In the closing years of the 20th century, rapid changes in transportation infrastructures (faster and cheaper means of transportation – lowcost airlines) accompanied by greater mobility (people looking for better working conditions), as well as the wider circulation of ideas beyond national borders enabled by the Internet revolution, have led to a generalized hybridism (interracial marriages, multicultural patterns of belief, world economic exchange by means of media – tools such as E – bay) have complicated what was once considered "identity" . Cultural characteristics such as ethnicity, language, gender, region, age, class and religion, which once formed the core structure of national identity, are no longer fixed realities. And anyone with a computer and internet connection can buy original Chinese products directly from Chinese suppliers with a click of the mouse.

However, Edward Said points out that culture means all those practices, like the arts of description, communication, and representation that have relative autonomy from the economic, social and political realms and that often exist in aesthetic forms, one of whose principal aims is pleasure (Said, 1993: xii). That is despite the fact that culture is under the influence of politics and the economy, it also has its own special features which is different from the economic, social and political realms. Like fashion, politics and economy operate on the superficial layers of culture, while the deeper core, less exposed to rapid change, is formed by value, beliefs and patterns of behavior, firmly rooted in the history of territories. Thus, Arif Dirlik's *Post - revolutionary Atmosphere* contemplates China's economic success as originating from a mixture of a strong sense of national cultural identity deeply grounded on Confucianism as an important foundation (Dirlik, 1999: 259). The following lines illustrate the importance of situating cultural development within a wider historical field.

Ever since the Opium War of the 1840s, writes Liang Qichao (梁启超) in "An overview of China's evolution in the past 50 years", China has undergone three stages of Westernization: economic, political and cultural, each corresponding to local movements: the Qing Restoration, the Reform Movement of 1898 (including the Constitutional Reform of 1905, the Revolution of 1911) and the May 4th New Culture Movement (Liang Qichao, 1984: 833 – 834).

In his article "May 4th Style Anti - traditional Thinking and the Crisis of Chinese Consciousness" (1988), Lin Yusheng distinguishes between two different concepts in the relationship between May 4th and Chinese tradition. In his view, the May 4th Movement is anti - tradition at the level of "thinking content", but not at the level of "thought mode", where it follows Chinese tradition. In this perspective, learning from the West would not necessarily cause the break – up of Chinese cultural tradition. The level of "thought mode" is displayed in the following two points. First, in the "practical rationality" of Chinese tradition, which consists in "the organic relation with transcendence and connotation of reality" (Lin Yusheng, 1988: 158). This view does not seek to surpass the nature of true phenomena, because the meaning of transcendence is connoted in real life. Inherited from representative characters of May 4th Movement, this mode of thinking owes much to Confucius, as illustrated in his saying "while you don't know life, how can you know about death?" (Confucius, 2011: 241).

The second point is the fact that although the spirit of May 4th Movement contains a kind of special sense of mission for Chinese intellectuals, this responsibility is directly linked to traditional Confucianism, where intellectuals were supposed to be "the first to bear hardships, and the last to enjoy comforts" (先天下之忧而有，后天下之乐而乐) and "not only concern themselves with personal affairs but the affairs of the state and the world" (家事、国事、天下事，事事关心).

Finally, in the 21st century the global scenario of Western economic crisis, people's disillusion with politics, and the decline of the power of nationstates, global economies are more and more dependent on communication systems, and economic attention is now set on the relocation of powerstructures. The Beijing Olympic Games of 2008 marked the entrance of China into the global system. Entering in the new era of Reform and Opening to the outside world, the majority of Chinese people are more concerned with economic issues and their living standards, than with politics and political reform, and many begin to see that the incorporation of some foreign cultural elements as beneficial for China's development. In an effort to situate China in this global panorama, the multidimensional model of cross – cultural research put forward in the following chapter examines the relationships between Chinese and Western cultures as seen through artistic translations and adaptations.

REFERENCES

[1] Cao Shunqing and Huang, Wenhu. Aphasia: from Literature to Art (失语症: 从文学到艺术) [J]. Literature and Art Studies, 2013 (6): 33 - 40.

[2] Cao Shunqing. The Discourse of Chinese Literary Theory and the Dialogue between Western Literary Theory and Chinese Literary Theory [J]. Journal of Zhejiang University (Humanities and Social Sciences), 2008 (1): 123 - 130.

[3] Cassell C. and Johnson P. Action research: Explaining the diversity, in Human Relations [M]. Tavistock Institute © SAGE Publications London, 2006.

[4] Clarke J. J. Oriental Enlightenment: The Encounter between Asian and WesternThought [M]. London and New York: Routledge, 1997.

[5] Cordier Henri. La Chine en France au XVIII - e siècle [M]. Translated by Tang Yuqing. Shanghai: Shanghai Bookstore Publishing Press, 2006.

[6] Damrosch David. How to Read World Literature? N J: Wiley - Blackwell Publishing. 2009: 105 - 124.

[7] Étiemble René. Do you know China? [M]. Translated by Xu Jun and Qian Shusen. Zhengzhou: Henan People's Publishing House, 1994.

[8] Fang Han - wen. The History of Eastern and Western Comparative Literature (东西方比较文学史) [M]. Beijing: Peking University Press, 2005.

[9] Frankel Han H. The Flowering Plum and the Palace Lady: Interpretations of Chinese Poetry [M]. New Haven: Yale UP, 1976: 68 - 72.

[10] Gergen K. Social construction in context [M]. Sage Publication, 2005.

[11] Grant S. and Humphries M. Critical Evaluation Of Apreciative Inquiry [J] Action Research, 2006 (4).

[12] Haar Van Der, D. A Positive Change. A Social Constructionist Inquiry into the Possibilities to Evaluate appreciative Inquiry [D]. Master Thesis, Tilburg University, 2002.

[13] Hegel Georg Wilhelm Friedrich. Lectures on the philosophy of world history: introduction, reason in history [M]. New York: Cambridge University Press, 1975.

[14] Huang Alexander C. Y. Two Centuries of Cultural Exchange [M]. New York: Columbia University Press, 2009.

[15] Li Qingben and Jinghua Guo. Translation, Cross - cultural Interpretation, and World

Literatures ［J］. CLCWeb：Comparative Literature and Culture，2013（6）.

［16］ Li Qingben. Multi – Dimensional Models of Cross – cultural Interpretation（跨文化阐释
的多维模式 ）［M］. Beijing：Peking University Press，2014.

［17］ Li Qingben. Cross – cultural Interpretation and Refactoring of World Literature.（跨文
化阐释与世界文学的重构）［J］. Shandong Social Sciences，2012（3）：43 –48.

［18］ Li Weimin. The Criticism History of Shakespearian Plays in China（中国莎士比亚批评
史）［J］. Beijing：China Drama Press，2006.

［19］ López – VarelaAzcárate，Asunción. Ed. Intermedial Studies and World Literatures ［J］.
Journal of Comparative Literature and Aesthetics. Vishvannath Kaviraja Institute of Comparative Literature and Aesthetics，Orissa，India，2013（36）：1 –30.

［20］ Said Edward W. Orientalism ［M］. New York：Vintage，1978.

Chapter 4

Cross–cultural Topographical Semio–spaces: the Example of China Hong Kong

As indicated in the introductory chapter to this research, in *Rhetoric of the Image*, one of the most prominent figures in semiotics, Roland Barthes, indicated that the differences between denotation and connotation have a clear ideological function. In *The Photographic Message*, Barthes specifies that every reproduction has a denoted message focused on the object being represented and a connoted message constituted by the viewer's culturally informed projections onto the image (1977: 17). In this sense, maps perform a form of bricolage, in Levi – Strauss' terms, re – imagining cartographies as Guy Debord did in *The Naked City*.

Debord sought to semiotically highlight the role of institutional power in creating the experience of the city, in this case Paris. Debord criticized the capitalist society of his time by describing the city as naked, both in the text and in the maps he used as illustrations. In semiotic terms, Debord's maps do not fulfil their paradigmatic purpose, predicated on the translation of textual cohesion to the visual field. Thus, like Barthes himself, Debord also shows the parasitic rationalizing of the image, which builds on a connoted message. The following lines explore similar techniques in a contemporary work. Dung Kai – cheung's novel *Atlas: The Archaeology of an Imaginary City*.

Playing an irreplaceable role for the whole speedy development in East Asia,

Hong Kong of China is an example of multi-cultural cosmopolitan urban centre in the Pacific Rim with strong ties with the Atlantic. However, with regards to mainland China, Hong Kong has always held a marginal position, carrying multiple marginal labels. In recent years, Hong Kong of China has been struggling to move beyond its Chinese/Western identities, simultaneously searching its own native insular self. This is shown in the way contemporary intellectuals approach China Hong Kong's memory. Although Rey Chow describes the Hong Kong situation as namely, "the struggle between the dominant and the subdominant within the 'native' culture itself " (Chow, 1992: 153), I would like to argue that Dung Kai – Cheung does not engage in the sort of radical anti – colonial, nationalist discourse that could be read through the lens of *The Empire Writes Back*. Rather, he seeks a new form of anti – colonial discourse which advances a reconciliatory cosmopolitan vision of multicultural coexistence in a marginocentric city.

Regarded as the "Oriental Pearl" of the Asia – Pacific, the city of Hong Kong of China has been playing an irreplaceable role in the speedy development of East Asia. Possibly, an important reason for Hong Kong's centrality lies, paradoxically, in its unique marginal geography. As a coastal Pacific city with rapid economic development, Hong Kong has generally been regarded by western economists as a strategic location at the Pacific Rim.

China Hong Kong, whose name in Cantonese means "Fragrant Harbour", is si-tuated at the South – Eastern tip of the mainland of China, 60km East of Macau on the opposite side of the Pearl River Delta. It is surrounded by the South China Sea on the East, South, and West, and at the North borders the Canton Province of Mainland China over the Shenzhen River. Its total area is beyond 1100 square km, including Hong Kong Island, the Kowloon Peninsula, as well as over 200 offshore islands.

Hong Kong of China has always been contemplated as a special city with multi – marginal labels. The region, first specialized in fishing and salt production, flou-rished as a regional trading port as early as the Tang dynasty (618 – 907). In the 16th century, Portuguese merchants began trading in southern China, particularly Macau. This was followed by clashes between China and Portugal, leading to prohibitions of foreign settlement in the territory. Hong Kong of China received an early form of political marginalization at the outbreak of the First Opium War (1839 – 1842) when the Qing dynasty refused to support the opium imports of the British Empire and their defeat resulted in the occupation of China Hong Kong Island by British forces in 1841. The city was first ceded as part of a ceasefire agreement and the following year the Treaty of Nanking confirmed the perpetual cession to the United Kingdom of Great Britain and Ireland (Courtauld, 1997: 38 – 58). The British established a Crown colony founding the City of Victoria. Following the Anglo – French victory after the Second Opium War, the colony was expanded to include Kowloon Peninsula (south of Boundary Street, Hong Kong City) and Stonecutter's Island under the Convention of Beijing in 1860. In 1898, under the Convention for the Extension of China Hong Kong Territory, Britain obtained the lease of Lantau Island, the area north of Boundary Street in Kowloon up to Shenzhen River and over 200 other outlying islands, having control of the entire region which acquired a free port status, attracting immigration from mainland China as well the Pacific.

Hong Kong of China became doubly marginalized with a racially segregated society under British colonial policies. Chinese population in Hong Kong had no political representation in the British colonial government, and laws, such as the Peak Reservation Ordinance prevented ethnic Chinese from acquiring houses in reserved areas. British colonists vigorously advocated the advancement of Western culture in Hong Kong, imposing sheer racial discrimination with the intention of eliminating the inborn and inherent national and local elements. The UK launched a large-scale cultural colonization in what refers to language, life styles, institutions and laws. However, the British did not really intend to assimilate the little island, so far away from Europe, into their own culture. Rather, regarding Hong Kong as nothing but a facility for trade with the orient, the UK tried to westernize Hong Kong's culture, diluting its national awareness in order to consolidate colonial rule. As Edward Said has explained, the Orient was seen as

vulgar and backward as compared to the more sensible and advanced Western civilization (Said, 1978: 300).

Further marginalization occurred when, as part of a general Pacific campaign during World War II, the Japanese launched an assault on Hong Kong on
the morning of 8 December 1941. The Governor surrendered the city after 18
days of fierce fighting against the invasion even though he had declared the
Crown Colony a neutral zone. Hong Kong's occupation by Japanese forces lasted
over three years until Japan's surrendered at the end of the Second World War.
Due to starvation, mass executions, and forced deportation for slave labour to
mainland China, Hong Kong decreased from 1. 6 million in 1941 to 600, 000
in 1945, when Britain resumed control of the colony, recovering after 1949
with the inflow of political migrants from mainland China after the establishment
of the People's Republic of China that year.

When the Kuomintang or Chinese National Party retreated to China Taiwan
in 1949 after its defeat by the Communist Party during the Chinese Civil War,
Hong Kong became a public sphere open to the free debate between both sides of
the China Taiwan Strait. Because of this situation, the city was doubly marginalized
as in – between Chinese regimes, remaining a British colonized enclave. A boundary
zone was created to prevent potential attacks from communist China. In the 1950s,
the territory became part of the so – called Four Asian Tiger economies under rapid
industrialisation.

Marginalized by both the Chinese and the British, Hong Kong of China
became a major global trade hub and financial centre in Asia – Pacific in the 1970s,
being reclassified in 1983 as a British Overseas Territory. Negotiations with China
concluded in the 1984 Sino – British Joint Declaration, and Hong Kong was
f inally transferred back to China in 1997, becoming a "Special Administrative
Region", able to retain free –market economy, British Common Law as well as
Hong Kong's, and independent representation in international organizations
(Wiltshire, 1997: 148; Liu, Wang and Chang, 1997: 291)

However, if Hong Kong was marginalized because of historical circumstances, nowadays it functions as an international cosmopolitan city as well as a Chinese national city with local characteristics, involving particular geographical, political and cultural factors.

Prior to the 1970s, historians saw the West as a homogeneous block, a kind of transnational cultural swarm that shared the same colonial aims. Other territories, such as China, were constructed as simplified abstractions of generalizations projected on them, with all diversity marginalized. From the medieval period, the Western imagination contemplated China as a mythical empire. In his Book of *Wonders*, Marco Polo defined some characteristics that remain unchanged for centuries in the European representation of China as a distant world of luxury, refinement and exoticism. After the fall of the Mongolian empire, which had managed to unify part of the vast territory linking Europe and Asia, the lack of direct contact between the two ends of the Eurasian continent contributed to the reification of these imagined realities.

It was not until the 16th century when the Portuguese Route led by Vasco da Gama to the coasts of India and China brought East and West into contact once more. Ideas, as well as different trading products, were circulated along this route. For centuries, besides the trading routes, Christian missionaries were the maximum exponent of the cultural relations between the Chinese Empire and Europe. The Jesuits became intercultural agents, being introduced to the imperial court and sharing a privileged place with Chinese officials and intellectuals, learning the language and history and translating the Confucian classics. Confucianism arrived in Europe transformed in a moral philosophy that anticipated the values of Christianity (Zhang, 1988: 118).

A significant number of historical processes that affected China's modern history were only noticed in their relation to the presence of the foreign countries on the China coast. Cultural aspects were given more weight than political and economic factors and, for example, it was assumed that China's traditional culture was synonymous with Confucianism and with an attitude of closure and resistance to the influence of Western modernization (Zhang, 1988: 108 – 131).

The 1970s represented a challenge to these approaches with the appearance a new generation of historians and critical voices who focused on denouncing discourses of imperialism in the context of the global protests against the Vietnam War. In the 1980s, John K. Fairbank inaugurated the discipline of Area Studies in the United States and played a major role in establishing the Centre for East Asian Research at Harvard University. One of his successors, Paul A. Cohen, challenged the assumptions of his tutor and proposed the revision of the validity and legitimacy of some of the categories applied to the analysis of Chinese history. One of the most important ideas introduced by Cohen is the fact that historical relations must be thought in terms of complex processes, rather than being the application of comparatist approaches that signal relations of imperialism, with one nation exercising power over others. Thus, he explains at the beginning of the book:

> My real quibble in this book is not with the disciplined, descriptive, application of terms like imperialism, impact, response, or even modern to specific, precisely delimited processes or phenomena that have emerged in the past century or so of Chinese history; what I object to is the use of these concepts as broad, overarching intellectual constructs purporting to tell us what was important—and by implication not important—about an entire period of historical time (Cohen, 1984: 4).

In his attempt to move beyond Western – centric paradigms, Cohen put forward one of the first interpretations of marginality based on littoral areas versus interior lands in China. In his 1974 "Littoral and Hinterland in Nineteenth Century China: The Christian Reformers", Cohen argued that two radically different cultural systems were produced in littoral and inner areas in China. In the littoral, Western (Christian) influence was felt more strongly, while the inner areas were more Chinese (Confucian) in their outlook. Falling into the very dialectic dichotomy he was trying to criticize, Cohen defended that the littoral zone was oriented toward foreign trade, maritime commerce and cosmopolitan ideas, while the hinterland was landlocked, agrarian and Sinocentric.

In the late 1990s, Andre Gunder Frank outlined a more holistic approach to the understanding of Chinese history in his volume *Reorient: Global Economy in the Asian Age* (1998). Similarly, in his book *The Great Divergence* (2000) Kenneth Pomeranz opted for comparative history in his criticism of Samuel Huntington, who had coined this expression in order to refer to the process by which the Western World became dominant over the East during the 19th century due to its most efficient forms of civilization. Pomeranz spoke of "a polycentric world without a dominant centre" (Pomeranz, 2000: 4).

The situation of Hong Kong was viewed from this perspective. In its early colonial period, the city was often labelled as uncultured by intellectuals from mainland China. This impression became even greater after it was ceded to the British. Although Hong Kong social circles had inherited the traditional Chinese culture from mainland immigrants, the culture there of was considered in authentic. For instance, this prejudice was even harboured by Lu Xun, the founder of modern Chinese literature with a wide influence as an overseas literary celebrity, as is evidenced by the mocking tone of his essay *A Brief Discussion of Hong Kong* published in 1927.

> However, Hong Kong is always a dangerous road. This can be proved with small issues. For instance, two pieces of news reported on Hong Kong's Circle Daily (...) News one makes us clear at a glance, Chinese are still hit by canes there (...) The second news is about the common occurrence of "body searching entanglement in Hong Kong." (Lu, Aug. 13, 1927)

Thus, while in the 1960s and 1970s, Hong Kong began to enjoy an economic boom which attracted world attention, it remained in a marginalized position in cultural terms, under its long-standing Chinese label as "the desert of culture". The city was a leader only in terms of economy, and did not received recognition from mainland China in other aspects such as politics, society and culture.

As Rey Chow has said, "The most exceptional thing about Hong Kong is its living in a crevice, as well as its awareness about its adulterated root. Hong Kong's post – colonial situation showed its shortage in both localism and post – modernism. (…) This post – colonial city (…) is compromisingly living in the crevice between the East and the West" (Chow, 1993: 101).

In spite of all these labels of marginalization, Hong Kong took a giant leap, beginning from a small fishing village with 5,000 people, continuing as a colonial enclave, to become a splendid international metropolis on the Pacific coast. This leap has been achieved in a historical process that has featured both shame and progress in the political wrestle between China and the UK, and under the dual influence of both Eastern and Western cultures.

In their paper "The Comparative Research on the Soft Power of Central Capital Cities in Six Provinces of Mid – China" (2013), Li Qingquan and Zheng Jifeng use Joseph S. Nye's ideas that a country national power not only emerges from hard power structures such as the military, science and technology, economy and so on, but also includes "soft power", fundamentally made up of culture. In cities, soft power is established in the intangible factors like the city culture, government services, social harmony and cohesion, education and innovation abilities, and the city's influence by means of its visibility, including image transmission etc (Li and Zheng, 2013: 473). In particular, "influence ability" is the key referencing factor to evaluate a cosmopolitan city.

Based on its economic strength, a city's ability to influence is a relative concept and a dynamic process as well. There are different index evaluation systems focusing on cosmopolitan and global cities. The Global Cities Index GCI was launched in 2008 by the North – American journal Foreign Policy in conjunction with the Chicago – based consulting firm A. T. Kearney and the Chicago Council on Global Affairs. GCI is applied to examine a comprehensive list of cities on every continent, measuring how globally engaged they are across 26 metrics in five dimensions: business activity, human capital, information exchange, cultural experience, and political engagement (*Global Cities Index and Emerging Cities Outlook*, 2014: 2). From its apparent marginality, Hong Kong has maintained stable fifth

- rank position in the GCI since 2008, an index featuring cites that serve as hubs of growth and global integration.

The Globalization and World Cities Research Network, commonly abbreviated to GaWC, at the Geography Department of Loughborough University, focuses on external relations among world cities based upon their international connectedness through four categories of advanced producer services: accountancy, advertising, banking/finance, and law. The GaWC inventory identifies three levels of global cities and several sub-ranks, "Alpha" world cities (with four sub-categories), "Beta" world cities (three sub-categories), "Gamma" world cities (three sub-categories) and additional cities with "high sufficiency" or "sufficiency" presence. Since Hong Kong kept its prominence as a major global trade hub and financial centre in Asia-Pacific for years, it has been ranked as a leading Alpha + world city.

Indeed, research indicates that many factors combine to make a city and its f inancial centre competitive. In the Global Financial Centres Index (GFCI 16th-edition), factors are grouped in five broad areas of competitiveness: Business Environment, Financial Sector Development, Infrastructure, Human Capital and Reputational and General Factors. GFCI 16 shows that New York, London, Hong Kong and Singapore remain the top four global financial centres of the world, with Hong Kong only 21 points behind them. The GFCI also developed a survey to ask respondents which centres they consider likely to become more significant in the next few years. Five of the top ten are in the Asia – Pacif ic region, and Hong Kong receives the most mentions (The Global Financial Centers Index 16, 2014: 2, 4, 8).

Hong Kong's GRP and per-capita GRP ranked the 35th and 7th respectively in the world in the 2013 statistics released by the International Monetary Fund (IMF), and was ranked third in the Global Financial Centres Index published by the City of London Corporation in 2013. Hong Kong is also the third largest recipient of Foreign Direct Investment (FDI) according to The World Investment Report released by the United Nations Conference on Trade and Development

(UNCTAD) in 2013 - 2014. The city has also been named the freest market e-conomy by the Heritage Foundation Index of Economic Freedom (http: // www. heritage. org/index/country/hongkong). In short, while Beijing enjoys excellence as a cultural city both in China and abroad, Hong Kong is a free inter-national commercial metropolis where its central cosmopolitan characteristics prove lively and particularly prominent as a major global trade hub and financial centre standing in Asia - Pacific.

More than other cities, port cities take on more diverse miscellaneous cul-tural features derived from their being transit territories. Besides, as a century - old colonial city, Hong Kong of China has an unimaginably complicated struc-ture of residents. There are natives, mainland Chinese, Taiwanese as well as for-eigners from the UK and various other countries. Meanwhile, all kinds of cul-tures, modern and traditional, eastern and western, are interactive in the u-nique heterogeneity of its urban space. Compared to some regional cultures in mainland China, the culture of Hong Kong is obviously more open and mixed, which is the result of both geographical position and political ideology. Hong Kong's history has absorbed the merits of many cultures, and yet developed its own patterns as an international metropolis.

Marginalization and centralization are the two most prominent features of Hong Kong. Seemingly contradictory, they are actually dependent on each oth-er. With the discussion of post - colonialism, marginality became endowed with more positive connotations, functioning as a bridge between two worlds. Mar-ginal cultures, like individuals, can be contemplated as "exiles" in transit, esca-ping categorization in particular historical periods. Living between two cultures can be, from the perspective of communication studies, enriching. The separa-tion from one's roots may allow the emergence of cosmopolitanism and broader horizons and perspectives as well as the consolidation of creativity and innovation as counter forces against static positioning (Rogers, 2002: 179 - 190). Accord-ing to Leo Lee, from a cultural perspective, though China Hong Kong has been marginalized, this does not mean that it has been disadvantaged, or its relationship be completely summarized as a post-colonial situation. Lee adds that China Hong Kong's identity cannot be explained totally by commercial theories:

> Perhaps the features of Hong Kong culture lie in its "heterogeneity", as it exists between the edges of several cultures, including China, America, Japan and India, but is free from their dominance. Even, without the need to play by the rules, the culture of Hong Kong can create some extraordinary splendour out of its diversity (Lee, 1995: 79 – 80).

On the negative side, this heterogeneity is one of the reasons why Chinese scholars continue to argue that "it has been difficult for Hong Kong to establish a historical and political identity" (Lee, 2003: 152 – 161).

According to Stuart Hall (1990), identity is not formed naturally, but constructed in relation to different historical, socio – cultural, political and economic appeals. To Hall, identity is a process, a sort of state of motion that includes alteration, translocation, eradication, assimilation and resistance; imagined and reproduced in different contexts. One of such contexts is the artistic domain. In the case of fiction, the literary work may reflect a country's history, culture and social ethos in a particular space – time, and sometimes in relation to the author and involving various factors such as class, gender, races as well as personal taste and shared cultural values.

Identification is not simply a natural mark, but something of a socialized label, related to a field of power, and constructed by multiple interrelations between the internal and the external, the subject and the object, the centre and the rim.

The term habitation means to locate a body in place. This may be transitory, a temporary placement or a more permanent settlement. "When I inhabit a place—whether by moving through it or staying in it—I have it in my actional purview. I also hold it by virtue of being in its ambience: first in my body as it holds onto the place by various sensory and kinaesthetic means, then in my memory as I 'hold it in mind'" (Casey, 2002: 687). Thus, the identity of a community, like those of a person, is mapped. Their mapping requires a spatial dimension, that is, an experiential and sensory body, as well as a record (history) of its temporal existences. Complicated hybrid identities yield paradoxical forms of non-unified existence, with diverse temporalities that render their telling fluid and provisional. This is the case of Hong Kong and of Dung Kai-cheung's Atlas: The Archaeology of an Imaginary City, a book that provides an imaginary map of the annihilated history of Victoria City (Hong Kong is never named in the story). The author explains that:

> No matter whether we understand them from the perspective of teleology or of utilitarianism, and no matter how scientifically and with what exactitude they are produced maps have never been copies of the real world but are displacements. In the end, the real world is totally supplanted in the process of displacement and fades from human cognition (Dung, 2012: 10).

Atlas: The Archaeology of an Imaginary City presents a China Hong Kong whose transient existence threatens disappearance. The book was conceived in the 1990s as the transfer of the city from Great Britain to the People's Republic of China was close. Indeed, as Ackbar Abbas has indicated, "part of the meaning of colonia-lism in Hong Kong is that the city can neither identify nor break with the past. Neither continuity nor discontinuity is available, only an appearance of continuity that is already discontinuous" (Dung, 1998: 300).

Although Rey Chow describes the Hong Kong situation as namely, "the struggle between the dominant and the subdominant within the 'native' culture itself" (Chow, 1993: 153), I would like to argue that Dung Kai-Cheung does not engage in the sort of radical anti-colonial nationalist discourse that could be read through the lens of The Empire Writes Back. Rather, he seeks a new form of anti-colonial discourse which advances a reconciliatory cosmopolitan vision of multicultural coexistence in a marginocentric city.

Dung Kai-cheung's understandings on the relations between territorial space and power are displayed in the book's impossible attempts to map China Hong

Kong's history and locate its movable identities. The author believes that "the map concretely shapes our imagination on space/ territory and time/history". In semiotic terms, a map is an iconic sign, it represents by means of similarities with the real. Thus, it cannot be separated from the concept of territory. "A map is neither the evidence of objective facts, nor only a tool to record the territory division. Map – drawing itself is the 'behaviour' of possessing one land, because the map is an effective practice for rulers to execute their power in the first place" (Dung, 1998: 154 – 160).

Indeed, cartography has long been imperative in understanding how civilisations have conquered, settled and shaped territories. Maps visualise the illusory spatial limitations of nations, often attempting to erase the layers of connected histories by creating invented boundaries. In this sense the geopolitics of disputed borders is informed by a biopolitics of identity practices. And this is precisely what Dung Kaicheung's work challenges: the semiotic practices embedded in representation, either by means of icons (maps) or symbols (discourse).

Atlas: The Archaeology of an Imaginary City charts what Ackbar Abbas has termed, following Michel Foucault's idea of heterotopias, "spaces of disappearance", countersites where Hong Kong's conflicting histories, Chinese and colonial, are contested and deconstructed by new ways of overlapping mapping and storytelling: "A verbal collection of maps" (Dung, 2012: xvii). Inspired by Foucault's concept of archaeology, Atlas is divided in to four parts: theory, the city, streets and symbols. Each part should be perhaps regarded as an independent location or place that, at the same time, penetrates the others. The city is shown as a "non – place", a space of transience (Augé, 1995) at the intersection of the telling of 50 spatial topoi. The final micro – essay, number 51, flings the reader back into the "Orbit of time".

The work, hardly a novel, does not follow along the fictional tradition that includes characters and their interactions, thus conform a plot narrated under a given point of view and discourse. Instead, unnamed archaeologists decipher fragments of lost cartographies, histories and signs. Dung Kaicheung maps the city as a discursive practice, as Henri Lefebvre and Michel de Certeau signalled from the point of view of critical urban theory. As spatial enunciation, the stories of the city express a practice which is not limited to telling. Rather, the telling constructs the city because its spatial dimensions, its body, is produced and re-produced through the human subjects that inhabit and move in it (de Certeau, "The Practice of Everyday Life", 1984: 84). Thus, as Heidegger already no-ted, the creation of place occurs through being in place (Dasein), that is, through movement, interaction and telling.

Interactions with places are not restricted to present actions and sensorial ex-periences of human communication and cooperation. They also occur in the form of creative projections: in remembering, imagining and telling. As such, places exist in temporal intersections that can follow successive linear patterns as conven-tional narratives, or overlap in a simultaneity of existences that allow a multiplici-ty of voices to speak simultaneously as the most avant-garde narratives of the 20th and 21st centuries.

Writing for the Los Angeles Review of Book in 2013, Sophie Kalkreuth in-dicates that the book captures Hong Kong as a paradoxical place of transit and in-betweenness, a "liminal place and its somewhat uncertain ' both/and', 'neither this nor that' sense of identity." (n/p) She adds that "in contrast to mainland Chinese cities, where the sense of place is palpable, pungent, inescap-able as the morning smog, Hong Kong—however hectic and densely popula-ted—is also characterized by a certain sense of vacancy", a vacancy captured by Dung Kai-Cheung who in the preface of his book indicates that "Hong Kong has been a work of fiction from the beginning." (Dung, 2012: xi).

Indeed, the name Hong Kong appears only in brackets, while Victoria City remains one of its archaeological shadows. The introduction explains:

> It is a fictional account of the City of Victoria (Hong Kong), a legendary city that
> has disappeared, written from the perspective of future archaeologists who reconstruct the
> form and facts about the city through imaginative readings of maps and other historical
> monuments [...] It is about the invention of a city through mapping and its reinvention

through map reading (Dung, 2012: xix – xx).

Each one of the 50 micro – essays deepens and complicates Dung Kai – Cheung's premise. Each piece overlaps with others, adding information, sometimes contradictory, in an accumulation of layers. Atlas functions as a palimpsest of layers, a kind of fractal structure where boundaries and categories disappear, and with them, identity: "There is no actually existing entity that serves as evidence of boundaries between districts or countries. Therefore, we can say that the boundary is a fictional exercise of power." (Dung, 2012: xxi)

The first part of the book, "Theory" deals with these issues from an interdisciplinary perspective, fusing philosophical with geopolitics and history. Using an unreliable narrator with something of a dreamer, something of a historian, and something of the author himself, Dung Kai – Cheung ironically shifts his focus from the colonial past to the neo – imperial future. The cartographic concepts contested in this part break the linear order of discourse becoming Foucaultian echoes: counterplace, commonplace, misplace, displace, antiplace, nonplace, extraterritoriality, boundary, utopia, supertopia, subtopia, transtopia, multitopia, unitopia, omnitopia. Any attempt to fix meaning, define and give identity to Hong Kong becomes futile:

> […] we come to the conclusion that Hong Kong is also a commonplace. It follows that when every place has its commonplaces, each of these places loses its distinctive character and becomes simply a common place. No place can transcend itself to attend an eternal and absolute state. When each and every place reiterates its existence through common means, replicating one another's commonality and vainly attempting to raise this commonality to the highest degree its repetitive self – affirmation may end up as a stale convention. This is the reason that modern maps of high precision lack imagination (Dung, 2012: 6).

If the first section suggests that "Theory" cannot explain China Hong Kong, in the second section "The City" abandons abstract space in order to situate itself "in place". For "Identity of place is as much a function of intersubjective intentions and experiences as of the appearances of buildings and scenery, and it refers not only to the distinctiveness of individual places but also the sameness between different places" (Relph, 1976: 44). This argument for the importance of personal and subjective experiences of place provides an additional map of Hong Kong as a living environment. "There are as many identities of place as there are people" (Relph, 1976: 45), so that any narrative of a place needs to integrate various layers of diverse subjectivities. "It is not just the identity of a place that is important, but also the identity that a person or group has with that place, in particular whether they are experiencing it as an insider or as an outsider" (Relph, 1976: 45).

A city, as a complex spatial entity, is also composed of many places, architectures, interactions, routes, signs, representations, memories, imagination. Michel de Certeau imagines walking itself as a gesture of enunciation: "the act of walking is to the urban system what the speech act is to language or the statements uttered" (Certeau, 1984: 97). A person who walks in the city appropriates the topography of the urban space. If the "Theory" section looks at the cartography from the abstract space as seen from above, "The City" zooms in on a series of grounded localized texts of those who inhabit the streets below. "The act of walking is to the urban system what the speech act is to language or to the statements uttered… It is a process of appropriation of the topographical system on the part of the pedestrian (just as the speaker appropriates and takes on the language), it is a spatial acting out of place" (Certeau, 1984: 97). Dung Kai-Cheung first situates "The City" as a mirage, as memories of the past, memoirs of early governors, anecdotes of other visitors, and fables of the city. The accounts oscillate between the real and the illusion even if the author has moved from the map to the plan.

A "plan" is a plane figure but also a design, a present visualization of future form. On the one hand it does not yet exist and is unreal, but on the other hand it is being designed and will be constructed. A plan is thus a kind of fiction, and the meaning of this fiction is inseparable from the design and blueprint. (Dung, 2012: 56)

— 119 —

In the same episode 20— "Plan of the City of Victoria", the author refers to Roland Barthes's reading of photographs, like maps and plans, iconic signs that show similarities with the real. But Dung Kai – Cheung does not pay attention to the lines of demarcation, those that separate the contours of things to render them visible. Instead, he is interested in the "indescribable punctum", the dotted lines that "represent the extent of projected reclamation work, that is to say, the direction of the city's future development" (Dung, 2012: 55).

As the flying birds of the Theory section transform into the parrots the tellingly populate The City section, the reader lands at Street level in the third part. Here, close up, the semiotic gaps between sign and referent are even wider, showing how interactions on street level can be fatal. This is the case of chapter 36, where a government sanitation officer falls in love with a local prostitute at Shui Hang Hau; or chapter 38, when a street changes names depending on the season; and of chapter 40, where a street is a square which in turn is a meeting place and a market, and where "itinerant performers would gather there at nightfall, casting divinations and telling fortunes, or singing and storytelling" (Dung, 2012: 115). When tracing street names in the book, the reader discovers that almost all the central areas are name in English almost without exception, revealing the process of colonization from its foundation, and keeping the colonial power embedded in the archives of the city's history. Naming is shown as an instrument of discursive power, from where there seems to be no escape. "Public Square Street" is visualized, following Jorge Luis Borges' frequent metaphor, as a labyrinth.

> Running around the plaza was a street in the shape of a square. This street did not have a beginning nor did it have an end, instead turning back in on itself. In addition, the four sides were of equal length, and the corners were at a uniform angle. The buildings along both sides of any one of these four streets were perfect matches for the buildings on the other three sides, whether in height, design, or order […] To enter the square street was to enter an absolutely predictable and calculable geometrical world, where there was only a single length and a single angle. However, it was actually the square street's regular and monotonous construction that made it a labyrinth from which it was

difficult to escape. In fact, a square street, wholly self-contained and with a name matching reality, has neither entrance nor exit. Therefore, the plaza enclosed by the square street was a sealed plaza, and the public nature of the street made it at the same time a private one (Dung, 2012: 116).

The above quotation refers to a square mapped as a street line, superimposed upon itself; that is an icon that repeats and builds upon itself, and whose regular repetitions create "a predictable world", just like the one constructed by linguistic signs. In this way, the secret plan of Atlas: The Archaeology of an Imaginary City, of which "Public Square Street" offers a Barthian photograph, brings the reader to the core and final Chinese box. "Signs", the smallest part of the book, lies within the place of "Streets", in turn encapsulated in the plan of "The City", mapped within the abstract space of "Theory".

After exhausting its "writing space", the book ends burying signs in "The Tomb of Signs" in chapter 50, while chapter 51 enters another dimension, "The Orbit of Time". The metaphor of "Public Square Street" is indeed a sign that stands for the map of the entire Atlas, and of the marginocentric character of Hong Kong, an insular city, whose identity, surrounded by the sea, is made up of fluid layers of waves of signs, routes, plans, maps. Dung Kai-Cheung not only maps the city, it captures its rhythm. Like in the contrapuntal musical composition known as fugue, "The Orbit of Time" signifies the book's "coda". It helps the reader understand that "marginocentric" is not a fixed structure, but a negotiated dynamic process.

> The city possesses a multi-temporality in itself, which consists of many pauses, currents and shifts that we experience in the course of what we learn in our everyday lives. Rhythm becomes relevant to the way that we understand subversive acts within the spatiality of the city. In this way, the city's rhythm constitutes an order and the coexistence of a series of different worlds and activities that are not centrally controlled or monitored top-down but are nonetheless being noticed and felt as the pulse that controls our lives, our movements and our actions in the city (Henri Lefebvre quoted in Helle Juul, 2012: 34).

REFERENCES

［1］ Ackbar Abbas. Hong Kong: Culture and the Politics of Disappearance ［M］. Hong Kong: Hong Kong University Press, 1997.

［2］ Ashcroft Bill; Griffith, Gareth and Tiffin, Helen. The Empire Writes Back ［M］. London and New York: Routledge, 1989.

［3］ Augé Marc. Non – Places: Introduction to an Anthropology of Supermodernity ［M］. Trans. John Howe. London Verso, 1995.

［4］ Barthes, R. Image, music, text ［M］. New York: Noonday Press, 1977.

［5］ Beaverstock Jonathan. V Smith, Richard. G and Taylor, Peter. J. A Roster of World Cities ［J］. Cities, 1999 (16): 445 – 458.

［6］ Calvino Italo. Invisible Cities ［M］. Trans. William Weaver. New York: Harcourt Brace Jovanovich, New York: Harcourt Brace & Company, 1972.

［7］ Casey Edward. S. Between Geography and Philosophy: What does it mean to be in the place – world? ［J］ Annals of the Association of American Geographers, 2001 (4): 683 – 693.

［8］ Cohen Paul A. Discovering History in China: American Historical Writing on the Recent Chinese Past ［M］. New York: Columbia University Press, 1984.

［9］ Cohen Paul. Littoral and Hinterland in Nineteenth Century China: the Christian Reformers ［M］//John Fairbank The Missionary Enterprise in China and America. edited. Cambridge: Harvard University Press, 1974: 197 – 225.

［10］ Courtauld Caroline, Holdsworth May and Vickers Simon. The Hong Kong Story ［M］. Oxford University Press, 1997: 38 – 58.

［11］ De Certeau Michel. The Practice of Everyday Life. Trans. Steven Rendall. Berkeley: University of California Press, 1984.

［12］ Debord G. The Naked City. Retrieved from http: //supralimen. wordpress. com/2011/ 05/18/feet – situationist – international – derive/.

［13］ Dung Kai – cheung. Atlas: The Archaeology of an Imaginary City ［M］. Trans. Dung Kaicheung, Anders Hansson and Bonnie S. McDougall. Columbia University Press, 2012.

［14］ Dung Kaicheung. Imaginary territory – Atlas series ［M］//Contemporaries. Hong Kong: three people press, 1998: 154 – 160.

［15］ Frank Andre Gunder. Reorient: Global Economy in the Asian Age ［M］. Los Angeles: University of California Press, 1998.

［16］ Kearney Andrew Thomas. Global Cities, Present and Future ［M］//2014 Global Cities Index and Emerging Cities Outlook, A. T. Kearney. Inc. 2014: 1-15.

［17］ Kearney Andrew Thomas. 2008 Global Cities Index ［M］//Foreign Policy. The FP Group, 2008.

［18］ Hall Stuart. Cultural Identity and Diaspora ［M］//Rutherford, Jonathan, ed. Identity: Community, Culture, and Difference. London: Lawrence and Wishart, 1990.

［19］ Juul Helle. Public Space: The Familiar into the Strange ［M］. Copenhagen: Arkitektur B, 2012.

［20］ Kalkreuth Sophie. Los Angeles Review of Books ［J］. January 12th, 2013: < htps: //lareviewofbooks. org/review/what - is - hong - kong - on - the - archaeology - of - an - imagina ry - city >.

［21］ Leo Lee. In Search of Hong Kong Culture ［M］. Guilin: Guangxi Normal University Press, 2003: 152-167.

［22］ Leo Lee. A Preliminary Discussion of the "Marginality" of Hong Kong Culture ［J］. Today, 1995 (2): 79-80.

［23］ Liu Shuyong; Wang, Wenjiong; and Chang, Mingyu. An Outline History of Hong Kong ［M］. Foreign Languages Press, 1997.

［24］ Lu Xun. A Brief View of Hong Kong ［J］. Threads, 1927 (13).

［25］ Pomeranz K. The Great Divergence: China, Europe and the Making of the Modern World Economy ［M］. Princeton: Princeton University Press, 2000.

［26］ Qatar Financial Centre. The Global Financial Centres Index ［J］. Long Financ, 2014 (9): 1-52.

［27］ Li Qingquan and Zheng Jifeng. The Comparative Research on the Soft Power of Central Capital Cities in Six Provinces of Mid - China ［M］//2nd International Conference on Science and Social Research (ICSSR 2013) 2013: 473-477.

［28］ < http: //www. atlantis - press. com/php/download_ paper. php? id = 7760 >

［29］ Rey Chow. Writing Diaspora: Tactics of Intervention in Contemporary Cultural Studies ［M］. Indiana University Press, 1993.

［30］ Rey Chow. Between Colonizers: Hong Kong's Postcolonial Self - Writing in the 1990's ［J］. Diaspora, 1992 (2): 151-170.

［31］ Relph Edward. Place and placelessness ［M］. London: Pion Limited, 1976.

［32］ Rogers. E. M. A History of Communication Study ［M］, Trans. Yin Xiaorong. Shanghai:

Shanghai Translation Publishing House，2002：179－190.

[33] Said Edward W. Orientalism ［M］. London：Routledge & Kegan Paul，1978.

[34] The Practice of the "One Country，Two Systems" Policy in the Hong Kong Special Administrative Region. issued by Information Office of the State Council，The People's Republic of China，2014（6）. ＜http：//www. scio. gov. cn/zxbd/wz/Document/1372867/1372867. htm ＞.

[35] The GaWC website：＜http：//www. lboro. ac. uk/gawc/world2012t. html ＞.

[36] Walter E. V. Placeways，A Theory of the Human Environment ［M］. Chapel Hill and London：The University of North Carolina Press，1988.

[37] Wayley Cohen P. The Sextants of Beijing：Global Currents in Chinese History ［M］. Nueva York：Norton，1999.

[38] Witshire Trea. Old Hong Kong. Vol. II：1901 － 1945. 5th ed ［M］. Form Asia Books，1997.

[39] Zhang Longxi. The Myth of the Other：China in the Eyes of the West ［J］. Critical Inquiry，1988（15）：108 －131.

Chapter 5

Cross-cultural Inter-semiotic Adaptation Western Adaptations of Chinese Classics

In the following section, I will focus on adaptation as a form of screen translation while maintaining a primarily semiotic approach. Henrik Gottlieb defines screen translation as the translation of transient polysemiotic texts presented on-screen to mass audiences. The label "transient" is included in order to keep the focus on the classical notion of "moving pictures". Accordingly, the notion screen translation includes translations of films displayed on "silver screens" in cinema theaters, broadcast televised material on TV screens, non-broadcast televised, for example DVD, material on TV or computer screens, online audiovisual material on computer screens. Compared with earlier notions of screen translation, the definition suggested above implies that screen translation is not necessarily interlingual—with dubbing, subtitling and voice—over as three dominant types. Catering for special audiences, subtitling for the deaf and hard of hearing and audio description (*intralingual* and *intersemiotic*, respectively), also qualify as screen translation, although I shall not refer to them in this chapter.

Recognizing the importance of Edward Said's 1978 work *Orientalism*, the chapter shows a desire to recover more positive approaches that endeavor to integrate Eastern culture and its influence upon the West, not in terms of power or domination, but in terms of cross-cultural encounters. In order to briefly exemplify the debate, the following chapter explores examples from Chinese folk and high culture. The first refers to Chinese folk stories adapted to film in the

West. The second, the multiple opera versions of Shakespeare's plays in the East.

Western scholars like to useinfluence/reception or center/periphery models to explain the cultural production mechanism of World Literature. This approach is a kind of refraction of West – centered theory, and may contribute, essentially, to the dissemination of Western civilization in other parts of the world. Under the severe pressure of dominant Western culture during the 20th century, those discourse rules and academic theories presented by the West have gradually become the controlling and universal powers. Oriental languages and traditions have had none or little voice on the international stage, becoming marginalized under labels such as "not scientific", "lack of methodology" and so on, and contemplated as very far from the Western of scientific modernity. In turn, such assertions have restrained innovation, development and oriental academic advancement, as many oriental scholars have turned to Western models in their search. It can be argued, however, that the establishment of their own patterns of cultural identification contributes to enhance national confidence, and the process of transplanting Western ideas directly into very different countries might fail or not achieve the desired results.

The "East – West" academic binary opposition, as in Rudyard Kipling's poem that "East is East, and West is West, and never the twain shall meet" is, in fact, a confrontation between civilizations that may encourage further forms of hostility and defiance. One obvious example is Georg Wilhelm Friedrich Hegel's discussion on China in his *Lectures on the Philosophy of History* (*Vorlesungenüber die Philosophie der Weltgeschichte*), originally delivered at the University of Berlin between 1821 and 1831. Hegel presented world history as following the dictates of reason and the emergence of a mature absolute spirit (Geist) in human nature, and itself the manifestation of an ultimate rational design for the world (understood as a superior intelligence or God). He contemplated human cultural and intellectual history as a manifestation of this spirit. According to Hegel, "World history [...] represents the development of the spirit's consciousness of its own

freedom and of the consequent realization of this freedom" (138) . In his classification, Hegel considered Chinese culture as a young culture in contrast to the
German one, which ranked at the top of human mature spirit. Hegel thought
that the reason for China's backwardness was this inner spiritual darkness, and
that Chinese people had not evolved from their original natural state of ignorance:
"World history is the record of the spirit's efforts to attain knowledge of what it is
in itself. The Orientals do not know that the spirit or man as such is free in themselves. And because they do not know that, they are not themselves free"
(54). In his article "Hegel's criticism of Chinese Philosophy" (1978), Young
Kum Kim indicates that Hegel upheld this European principle of centralism, placing the East as the antithesis of the West, and regarding Germanic culture as the
consummation of human history.

In today's world we have moved beyond this Eurocentric views, and now
the problem is to construct effective dialogue and communication beyond the
East – West dichotomy, a dialogue that also moves beyond Orientalist's positions
that criticize the dominance of the West. Recognizing the importance of Edward
Said's 1978 work *Orientalism*, I share with J. J. Clark a desire to recover more
positive approaches that endeavor to integrate Eastern culture and its influence
upon the West, not in terms of power or domination, but in terms of cross –
cultural encounters. My argument is that a multi – cultural system needs be imple-
mented. In the past, scholars tended to simply divide one complex situation only
into two sides in accordance with binary thinking modes. They would only investigate one side ignoring the other; or they would only pursue the simple and mechanical relationship between cause and effect. This manner of thinking is quite
alien to Chinese traditional dialectical thinking. Thus, Chinese scholars argue that
"the binary opposition distinctions between the strengths and weaknesses, the mainstream and edge, the elite and secular, will not include the diversified development trend between heterogeneous discourses" (Cao & Huang, 2013: 38).

As J. J. Clarke points out in his 1997 book *Oriental Enlightenment*, the
movement of appropriating of Western ideologies has been driven, in many ca-

ses, by Western demands, that is, external factors. On the other hand, the Western appropriation of Asian philosophies was caused by a "pervasive cultural disquietude, an uneasy awareness of fault lines running deep into the strata of European cultural life" (28). Clark argues that from the Renaissance to the Enlightenment "Europe underwent a profound transformation amounting to a radical discontinuity with its past" (30), and that this "painful void in the spiritual and intellectual heart of Europe" (34) combined with imperialism and global expansion led Europe to look outwards. Thus, while Asian integration of Western elements was moved by external factors, in the case of Europe the causes were related to the very spirit of rationalism, which led to industrialization but also to anxiety and self – doubt, a situation that became more serious in the 19th century with the expansion of the colonial spirit.

The unlimited expansion of the Western centralism in the age of global discourse has at least led to the following consequences: the inhibition of academic self – discovery and oriental creativity; the negation of possibilities for cooperation, innovation and cultural dialogue between the East and the West, making global knowledge myopic and deficient, and finally the consolidation of unequal relationships and inner prejudices between human cultures. Cao Shunqing indicates that four basic rules should be followed in order to encourage dialogues between the East and the West: independent dialogue principle, equal dialogue principle, and two – way interpretation, all of which seek "common ground while reserving differences", and heterogeneous complementary principles (Cao, 2008: 127 – 29). Such assertions challenge the stereotypical perception of the division, and even conflict, between East and West, between Western rationalism and Eastern intuitive thinking.

With over 5000 years of history, China retains a philosophic method and a problem – solving system with its own particular characteristics. These need to be practiced during the process of transmission and interpretation of Chinese culture to the world. In its cultural development, Chinese world outlook on subjects such as natural and human harmony, and its dialectic view of life and communal patriotism differ from the Western philosophical framework. These differences function as important theoretical sources for interpreting Chinese culture, worthy of being followed by those engaged in these discussions. Besides, for Chinese scholars or for those interested in Chinese cultural research, it is imperative to re-discover, reinterpret and re – express Chinese traditional and academic concepts, theories and methods, in order to build a proper interpretation paradigm with Chinese cultural characteristics, helping Chinese scholars rediscover their own voice and identity. In this way, China will not only know itself better, but the world will understand China better, and Chinese culture will experience better dissemination throughout the entire world. Such program will also encourage multi – cultural dialogues and create a global and richer critical research culture. Chinese scholars and media should strive to overcome cultural inequality and en-hance the spread of their own culture, methodologies and systems of thought.

Cultural dissemination is very different from the spread of objective know-ledge. During the process of communication, cultural information is subject to different visions and interpretations and, thus, inevitably changed. This muta-tion appears in obvious ways, as a result of conflict, collision, negotiation and compromise between different cultures. When influences enter a receiving cultur-al field, changes are introduced in both the producer and the receiver. Cultural migration is, in this way, a type of circular structure, always including at least a two – way variation (Li, 2012: 45).

The so-called cross-cultural model of interpretation means the use of national language, symbols and culture to dialogue with another national language, sym-bols and culture. It is a multi – dimensional model that differs from East – West dualism, where each entity was considered isolated and homogenous in a kind of linear plane study between A and B. The multi-dimensional model of cross – cul-tural interpretation attempts to re-examine the relationship between the East and the West in aspects such as knowledge dissemination and transmission. Thus, taking as example the circulation of literary texts and critical theory, cross – cul-tural interpretation struggles to situate in the map of East – West transactions, the dissemination of oriental discourse in the West. The theory also advocates the preservation of national cultural aspects, although integrating its local characteristics. It also contemplates culture dissemination in its historical perspective, from the ancient to the modern, taking into consideration the different rhythms present in Eastern and Western cultures. This model reads and interprets the world as a kaleidoscope of horizons of cultural pluralism.

The basic principle that this multi – dimensional system should follow is the inclusion of a paradigm based on local cultures with forms of blending with other histories and cultures, ideas and theories. Thus, the model promotes entering into the other's culture and accepting a plurality of views. The paradigm should also have a global outlook, ruling out particular forms of cultural hegemony and emphasizing cultural diversity. Academic institutions have a particular important role in promoting this plurality actively.

David Damrosch states in his book *How to Read World Literature* that third world countries will encounter the following three difficulties in promoting their nations' literature: firstly, a language not belonging to any of the major world languages, which becomes an obstacle for acceptance; secondly, the fact that their culture might not receive worldwide attention because of its relatively weak political and economic position, and third, in the case of literary works equipped with national particularities and unique cultural details, difficulties in cultural comprehension by foreign readers may result (Damrosch, 2011: 105 – 124). With a growing impact on global political and economic affairs, China is no longer contemplated as a third world country, but apparently, it still requires overcoming those three difficulties. Translation can solve the first difficulty; improving China's comprehensive national power contributes to dealing with the second; for the third difficulty, cross – cultural interpretation will serve as an effective strategy (Li, 2014: 69).

The multi – dimensional model of cross-cultural interpretation also advocates the change of the temporal dimension of Western hermeneutics into a global spatial dimension, rethinking the relationships between different nationalities and cultures at a global scale, and seeking cross – cultural understanding and dialogue. This inclusion of the spatial dimension means the acknowledgement and inclusion of national cultural differences. On this basis, pursuing an effective means for cross – cultural dialogue and understanding will be advocated in order to achieve pluralistic universalism.

David Damrosch's works on World Literature has been prevalent in global academia and produces great influence. He believes that a text becomes a work of world literature if it continues to remain vibrantly engaged in cultures beyond its sphere of origin. He feels that world literature is actually improved when it internationalizes the works' mode of circulation and challenges different cultures across time in a transnational hermeneutic dialogue. Such circulation can also take place in the form of adaptations to other media, as López – Varela has argued (2013). Thus, in the following lines I engage with two animated films produced by Walt Disney Company, *Mulan* (1998) and *Kung Fu Panda* (2008) which can be used as an example of the multi – dimensional model of cross – cultural interpretation.

The folk story of Hua Mu – Lan is known in every household in China. The animated filmic version of the story entitled *Mulan* was written by Robert D. San Souci and Rita Hsiao, directed by Tony Bancroft and Barry Cook, and produced by Walt Disney Company. The story is based in an ancient Chinese folk ballad, but Disney created a new image of the character Mu – Lan, devised to appeal to a wide audience around the world. *Mulan* was a huge success and earned huge profits for Disney productions as well as a flood of global praise at the time, with some American critics acclaiming it as the best of Disney's films. *New York Times* reads that "Disney takes a sledgehammer to the subject of gender stereotyping in *Mulan*, a film that not only breaks the cross – dressing barrier but also ratchets up the violence level for children's animation. [...] Though the plot and setting present exotic new opportunities for the filmmakers, the China of 'Mulan' has surprisingly little depth of field or background detail. The Great Wall and the Forbidden City are here, but so are a lot of empty spaces and scenes in which only one figure moves" (New York Times Jun. 19, 1998).

As years have passed, criticism on the movie has evolved. For example, Alex von Tunzelmann in his article "Disney's *Mulan* takes a hammer to a Chinese puzzle" writes that: "There is little historical evidence on Mulan and her time [...] Still, as Disney heroines go, Mulan herself is a clear improvement on the standard – issue drippy princess" (The Guardian Sept. 9, 2010).

With a global audience as its marketing target, a large number of modifications were made to the original Chinese folk *Ballad of Mulan* (木兰辞). The real Chinese folk ballad originated around in the Northern Wei dynasty of ancient China (386 – 536), and the original text of this poem comes from another work known as the *Music Bureau Collection* (乐府诗集), an anthology of lyrics, songs, and poems, compiled by GuoMaoqian during the 11th or 12th century.

In the Chinese ballad, Hua Mulan took her aged father's place in the army. She fought for twelve years and gained high merit, but she refused any reward and retired to her hometown instead. In Chinese, the ballad reads "阿爷无大儿, 木兰无长兄, 愿为市鞍马, 从此替爷征", which means "Father has no grown – up son, Mu – Lan has no elder brother. I want to buy a saddle and horse, and serve in the army in Father's palace" (Frankel, 1976: 68). Mu – Lan's filial piety and virtue are vividly presented. Thus, it conveys a very different ethos from the North – American person – oriented culture, which pays attention to the individual dignity and self – worth, rather than family and community values. This is portrayed in Disney's character, which actualizes her individual consciousness and her desire to realize her own achievements. As a result, the Chinese concept of filial piety and collective consciousness is greatly weakened. Instead, Disney enhances Mu – Lan's individual characteristics as a brave, independent female, thus addressing a Western audience in accordance with contemporary feminist values. For example, Mulan states in the film that "Maybe I didn't go for my father. Maybe what I really wanted was to prove I could do things right. So when I looked in the mirror, I'd see someone worthwhile"

(*Mulan* film script n/p). Those few words express clearly that Mulan replaces her father on the battlefield no longer for the sake of filial piety, but because she wants to prove herself a useful person. She pursues her own personal value and the honor of family and her country; filial piety reflected in the original ballad has completely been replaced.

By means of the adaptation in Disney's animated version, a story with strong traditional Chinese feudal consciousness can be accepted by audiences all over the world. The movie stages a cultural hybridization of individualism and collectivism, female obedience and women's liberation, filial devotion and two – way communication between father and daughter. Thus, this process of cross – cultural adaptation serves to achieve a form of global cultural transmission that appeals to almost everyone. Even if *Faye Wang writing for the Huffington Post* in January 31, 2015, says:

> I think it's not so much that the movie is bad; I personally like the movie a lot. It's more about culture differences. After all, *Mulan* wasn't even trying to preserve Chinese culture. It is a straight out American movie decorated with Chinese accessories to make it interesting and exotic. *Kung Fu Panda* did a much better job.

Kung Fu Panda is an animated action comedy film of anthropomorphic talking animals, produced by DreamWorks Animation. Directed by Mark Osborne and John Stevenson and written by Jonathan Aibel and Glenn Berger, the movie premiered in USA in 2008 and became one of DreamWorks' hits. *Kung Fu Panda* presents a combination of traditional Chinese cultural factors, especially Chinese 道, Dao philosophy, as exposed by the ancient Chinese philosopher Laozi (老子). The essence of "The Way", as Dao is translated, can be seen in the movie in the character of the Panda Po, and his aspirations to become a Kung Fu master. Po practices martial arts relentlessly, and experiences various failures, finally saving the lives' of his hometown relatives.

As in *Mulan*, a single hero or heroine are responsible for saving a group of people, a community, nation, or even the entire planet. The individual "I" is once more highlighted. The character of Po brings to mind many aspects of the culture of the United States: his dreaming nature and his pursuit of personal freedom and heroic values. As in *Mulan*, the Chinese story is adapted to the new cultural setting, combining the strengths of Chinese culture, while adhering to North American life style. Thus, we can say that *Mulan* and *Kung Fu Panda* do not simply belong to the culture of one country. They have become examples of cross – cultural phenomena, exemplifying a mixture of sometimes opposing ideas, combining old traditions and new interpretations from both East and West. However, it would be necessary to expose these cross – cultural processes in a clearer way so that people across the world become aware of the origins of the stories and of the diverse understanding of other cultures. In turn, this also brings awareness of one's own culture, stimulating both revival and innovative approaches within a given national perspective. In this way, *Mulan* and *Kung Fu Panda* have become the inspiration for other similar cultural products in China. This time the stories originate in local U. S. environments and become adapted to Chinese ways of thinking.

REFERENCES

[1] Cao Shunqing& Huang, Wenhu. Aphasia: from Literature to Art [失语症: 从文学到艺术] [J]. Literature & Art Studies, 2013 (6): 33 – 40.

[2] Cao Shunqing. The Discourse of Chinese Literary Theory and the Dialogue between Western Literary Theory and Chinese Literary Theory [J]. Journal of Zhejiang University (Humanities and Social Sciences), 2008 (1): 123 – 130.

[3] Clarke J. J. Oriental Enlightenment: The Encounter between Asian and WesternThought [M]. London and New York: Routledge, 1997.

[4] Cordier Henri. La ChineenFranceau XVIII esiècle [M]. Translated by Tang Yuqing, Shanghai: shanghai Bookstore Publishing Press, 2006.

[5] Damrosch David. How to Read World Literature? [M] N J: Wiley – Blackwell Publishing, 2009: 105 – 124.

[6]　Disney's Mulan Script. Compiled by Barry Adams during theater showings in 1998 < http：//www. imsdb. com/scripts/Mulan. html >.

[7]　Etiemble Rene. Do you know China? ［M］. Translated by Xu Jun& Qian Shusen. Zhengzhou：HenanPeople's Publishing House，1994.

[8]　Fang Han – wen. The History of Eastern and Western Comparative Literature ［东西方比较文学史］［M］. Beijing：Peking University Press，2005.

[9]　Frankel Han H. The Flowering Plum and the Palace Lady：Interpretations of Chinese Poetry ［M］. New Haven：Yale University Press，1976：68 – 72.

[10]　Hegel Georg Wilhelm Friedrich. Lectures On The Philosophy of World History：Introduction，Reason in History ［M］. Translated from the German edition of Johannes Hoffmeister from Hegel papers assembled by H. B. Nisbet. New York：Cambridge University Press，1975.

[11]　Li Qingben & Guo Jinghua. Translation，Cross – cultural Interpretation，and World Literatures ［J］. CLCWeb：Comparative Literature and Culture. 2013 （6）：< http：// dx. doi. org/10. 7771/1481 – 4374. 2358 >.

[12]　Li Qingben. Multi – Dimensional Models of Cross – cultural Interpretation （跨文化阐释的多维模式）［M］. Beijing：Peking University Press，2014.

[13]　Li Qingben. Cross – cultural interpretation and refactoring of World Literature （跨文化阐释与世界文学的重构）. Shandong Social Sciences，2012 （3）：43 – 48.

[14]　Maslin Janet. A Warrior，She Takes on Huns and Stereotypes. ［J］ New York Times，1998 （19）.

[15]　< http：//www. nytimes. com/movie/review? res = 9C00E3D91E3DF93AA25755C0 A96E958260 > ［16］Said Edward W. Orientalism ［M］. New York：Vintage，1978.

[16]　Tunzelmann Alex von. Disney's Mulan takes a hammer to a Chinese puzzle ［J］. The Guardian. 2010 （9）. < http：//www. theguardian. com/film/2010/sep/09/mula n – disne y – re el – history >

[17]　Wang Faye. How is Disney's Mulan perceived in China. ［J］. Huffington Post. 2015 （31）. < http：//www. huffingtonpost. com/quora/how – is – disneys – mulan – pe rc_ b_ 4314035. html >.

[18]　Wang Guowei. The Preface of Traditional Chinese Periodicals ［国学丛刊序］ ［M］//Edited by Xie Weiyang & Fang Xinliang. The Complete Works of Wang Guowei ［王国维作品集］，Hangzhou：Zhejiang Education Publishing House，2010.

[19] Young Kum Kim. Hegel's criticism of Chinese Philosophy [J] . Philosophy East and West, 28. 1978: 173 – 180 < http: //www. jstor. org/stable/1397741 >.

[20] Yue Daiyun. Status quo and the future of comparative Literature [比较文学研究的现状和前景] . Journal of Lanzhou University (Social Sciences) 2007 (6): 1 – 13.

Chapter 6

Cross-cultural Inter-semiotic Adaptation: Shakespeare in China

As I have shown in the previous chapter, Chinese classics are cross – culturally interpreted successfully in the West. Similarly, Western classics, such as Shakespeare's works, also obtain adapted cross – culturally as products in Chinese cultural industries. In *The Preface of Traditional Chinese Periodicals*, Wang Guowei affirmed that Chinese and Western mindset must prosper together or decline together (《国学丛刊序》"中西二学, 盛则俱盛, 衰则俱衰, 风气既开, 互相推助) (Xie & Fang, 2010). This statement illustrates the common desire by many Chinese scholars to find ways in which "the culture and literature between Chinese and West possesses the characteristics of being mutual awareness, complement and prove each other" (Yue, 2007: 10). Thus, the adaptation of Shakespeare's classics is possibly one of most important ones taking place in a Chinese context. The study of such cross – cultural adaptations has positive significance not only for development of literary theory, literary criticism and literary history, but also in that it promotes unusual forms of innovation with regards to the study of performance in general, and to Shakespeare's works in particular.

In his 1996 work, Zhang Xiaoyang refers to the general impact of Shakespeare on Chinese theatre and culture, and the convergence of Shakespearean and traditional Chinese drama on the Chinese stage. Each of these is treated in rather problematic ways. He claims that Shakespeare not only has had "an impact on the formation and development of modern Chinese theatre", but also "has entered into numerous domains of Chinese culture and exerted a widespread and profound influence upon them as well" (13), becoming "the most important and authoritative dramatic form in Chinese cultural circles today" (129). He also asserts that "the impact [of Shakespeare] has brought the decline of traditional Chinese drama to the point where it could die out completely as a feeble and decaying art with unfashionable beauty or survive through reform at the risk of losing its own distinctiveness" (129) (Zhang, 1996).

In 1943, the Shanghai Art Troupe staged *Three Daughters* edited by Gu Zhongyi according to Shakespeare's *King Lear* and to the Chinese traditional opera *The Story of Wong Bo – chuen*. In 1945, Kugan Troupe played *Deming Wang* adapted by Li Jianwu and based on Shakespearian *Macbeth* and Yuan Verse *The Orphan of Zhao*, renamed *Gone with the Hero*. The adaptation of the two plays, mainly follows stage design, where Shakespearian characters are turned into their Chinese counterparts, and combining a Shakespearian plot with a Chinese narrative. However, these changes allow Beijing Opera fans to understand the essence of Shakespeare's plays, now presented in a more familiar art form. As a consequence, such adaptations function as a bridge for Sino – foreign cross – cultural exchanges and interpretations.

Shakespeare's plots have inspired incredible work in the literature, fiction, theater, and cinema of China, China Taiwan, and Hong Kong. From the novels of Lao She and Lin Shu to Lu Xun's and Feng Xiaogang's martial arts films, Soviet – Chinese theater, and Chinese opera. Adaptations of Shakespeare have yielded a rich trove of transnational cross cultural imagery (Huang, 2009).

This chapter has traced a brief overview of the importance of mutual cross – cultural dialogue between East and West. Although Western influence is largely acknowledged in the East, with many examples coming from the world of academia where, in the case of Chinese scholars, theoretical sources are often drawn from Western models, the movement of knowledge from East to West has not been so clearly documented. Beyond the exploits of Marco Polo and the encounters brought on by Jesuit missionaries, little is known on the influence of Chinese culture in the West.

Furthermore, since the beginning of the 19th century, China's image among the international community has been misunderstood and misinterpreted. Typical views of the comprehension of Chinese thought have been extremely one – sided, as illustrated in appellatives such as "Yellow Peril", "Chinese Threat" and so on. These ideological biases are dominated by the Western prejudice against oriental cultural consciousness, lacking in perception and experience of the true China. Some Western scholars such as Etiemble Rene, and more recently, J. J. Clarke, have described how China's image had been mutilated and deformed in the West. However, for some Chinese scholars, this recognition is still the result of the prominence of a Eurocentric view (Etiemble, 1994).

The example of the adaptations mentioned in this book shows that it is very difficult to reconstruct appropriate Chinese images and ways of exporting Chinese culture to the West. The book also shows that Western models have greater success in adapting themselves to Chinese patterns. This reveals an unequal dialogical situation, where the cross – cultural journey across the world is not complete. My argument is that a balance should be reached, and that Chinese scholars should also rely on their own models in order to make their cultural voices heard.

An Overview of Shakespeare's Translations and Adaptations in China

William Shakespeare is a major figure in Western culture and has also had a great impact in China. His works have been adapted to multitude of genres and media, translated, adapted to television and film, or used in the videogames industry in the Internet. The adaptation of Shakespeare's plays for the Chinese stage constitutes an interesting place to engage questions of cross – cultural epistemologies. Therefore, I focus here on the differences between Chinese and Western drama and contextualize them as forms of semiotic cultural translation. By looking at the differences and similarities between dramatic conventions in

Shakespeare's time and traditional Chinese drama, I seek to explore the mechanisms of semiotic translation and adaptation between the two cultures. The main sources I have used for Shakespeare are Zhang Xiaoyang's (1996) *Shakespeare in China*, *A Comparative Study of Two Traditions and Cultures*, Murray Levith's (2004) *Shakespeare in China*, and Alex Huang (2009) *Chinese Shakespeares*. Regarding semiotics and drama, I use Antonin Artaud, John Gielgud, Vsévolod Emílievich Meyerhold, Konstantin Stanislavski and Anne Uberbeld among others. In particular, I focus on Shakespeare's political tragedies exemplified in *Hamlet*, and its comparison to the Chinese political scene as recounted in *The Orphan of the House of Zhao* (Zhao Shi Gu Er).

The late Qing (1839 – 1910) and early Republican (1911 – 1930) fascination with Anglo – European ideas and products encouraged the first biographical sketches of William Shakespeare in China. In 1894, Yan Fu wrote in *The Evolution of Nature*, that Shakespeare was an English poet and playwright whose works would spread far and wide among readers all over the world. However, Shakespeare's works did not appear in China, even in partial translation, until 1904, when Lin Shu and Wei Yi published their collaborative classical Chinese translation of Charles and Mary Lamb's *Tales from Shakespeare*. The first complete translation of a Shakespearean play appeared in 1921 when Tian Han's *Hamlet* (Hameng – leite) was published. In the 1920s, following the translations of Tian han, seven other translations of Shakespearean plays were published in China. By the 1930s, the Chinese fascination with Europe gave rise to the intensive translation of Western dramas, including the tragedies: *Mabeth* (three versions), *King Lear*, *Othello*, *Hamlet*, *Julius Caesar*; the comedies: *The Merchant of Venice* (three versions), *Twelfth Night* (two versions); and the romances: *The Tempest* (two versions). The 1940s and 1950s even more sophisticated translations of Shakespeare's plays appeared, such as a version of *Romeo and Juliet* (1944) translated by Cao Yu, the leading figure in modern Chinese theatrical circles; a version of *Timon of Athens* (1944) translated bu Yang Hui; Liu Wu Ji's translation of *Julius Caesar* (1944); Sun Da Yu's translation of *King*

Lear (1948); Fang Ping's translations of *Much Ado About Nothing* (1953) and *Henry the Fifth* (1955); Bian Zhi Lin's translation of *Hamlet* (1956); Wu Xing Hua's translation of *Henry the Fourth* (1957); and Fang Zhong's translation of *Richard the Third* (1959).

However, despite all these translations, Shakespeare was still unknown in the Chinese stage. Lin Shu's translation not only influenced many modern Chinese writers, but it also served as the stage script for the first Shakespeare productions in China before the May Fourth Movement (1913 – 1918). The earliest Shakespeare production with Chinese actors was held in 1902. It was a production of *The Merchant of Venice*, performed in English by the students of the Foreign Language Department, Shanghai St. John College. The main purpose of the performance was to promote the English study of the students, so it cannot be regarded as the first Shakespeare production in Chinese. The first one in Chinese was presented in 1913 by the New People's Society (Xin Min She), a dramatic organization in Shanghai. There were two Shakespearean productions in 1916: an adaptation of *Merchant* performed by the Yao Feng New Drama Troupe under the title *The Usurper of State Power*, and an adaptation of *Hamlet* called *The Instruction of Ghost*, presented by the Spring Willow Association. Before and during the May Fourth New Cultural Movement (1917 – 1929), more Shakespeare productions appeared on the Chinese stage. A very successful one was *Romeo and Juliet* in 1937, performed by the Shanghai Practical Drama Company in the Carlton Theatre under the direction of Zhang Min.

During the Cultural Revolution, both Western and Chinese cultural heritages were condemned as bourgeois and feudal. Chinese translation of the complete works did not come true until 1978, including all thirty – seven plays and the poems. It was well received by Chinese readers and has been regarded as the most authoritative Chinese version of Shakespeare's works, even if the unique style of Shakespearean language had to be neglected in favor of content. Some scholars, like Prof. Sun Da Yu insisted that it was a pity to translate blank verse with prose because readers would lose the beauty of the plays as poetic drama. Thus, in his translation of *King Lear* Sun Dayu tried to use a syllabic unit that he created to produce the effect of beat in Shakespeare's blank verse.

After the Cultural Revolution, China's first Shakespeare Festival, which was organized by The Research Society of China, the Chinese Dramatic Art Research Society, and the Beijing and Shanghai Drama Academies. It took place from 10 to 23 April 1986, and during this time more than two dozen versions of sixteen Shakespeare plays appeared in various stages. In addition, Shakespeare societies were founded in the mid – eighties. The first of these was the Shakespeare Society of Jilin Province in 1985. Professor Lin Tongji established a Shakespeare research library at Shanghai's Fudan University, and in 1984 Beijing's Central Academy of Drama created a special collection on Shakespeare materials for study in universities and drama schools. In 1993, Wuhan University sponsored the first International Conference on Shakespeare in China. The following year, Shakespeare Festival was held in Shanghai. Perhaps the most controversial of all Festival productions, however, was the first Taiwanese-PRC joint – venture offering, a play loosely based on *Hamlet* and titled *Shamlet*. In recent years, two feature films based on *Hamlet* have been produced: The Banquet (2006) and *The Prince of the Himalayas* (2006); the first one reinterpreted the structure of imperial China and emotions in *Hamlet*. *The prince of the Himalayas* was so popular in China that Mandarin – Tibetan huaju (spoken drama) stage versions based on the film, with the same cast and director, were staged in Shanghai and Beijing, thus crossing cultural boundaries and creating a new space for ethnic minority performers.

Drama and Cross – cultural reception: a semiotic analysis

As seen in a previous section of this volume, the analysis of drama concerns various elements, some of which have a subjective imprint (sender and receiver) while others can be considered more or less objective (the signs used, and the messages conveyed, the codes and languages, as well as the channel and con-text). There are also pragmatic elements (*processes of expression* and *reception*). Thus, first we must look at the *selection* of elements (characters, objects on stage, etc.), then their *organization* (*plot*, *story structure*) and final the *per-formance*. The levels of *content* and *expression* take the form of *beings* (charac-ters) and *actions* (their ways of speaking and behavior) with relationships estab-lished between them in a concrete spatiotemporal context.

Theatre contains various semiotic languages in its processes of expression : gestures, *prosody*, *kinesics* and *proxemics*, spoken language, music, noise, the location of the objects on stage, and so on. Dramatic codes such as stage di-rections and feedback from the director, the audience and other actors, also modify the process of expression during the performance. This feature impacts up-on the *cognitive*, *emotional* and *ideological perspectives*, and affects the pheno-menon of audience *identification* with the characters, so intimately linked to *ca-tharsis*.

At the level of *expression*, and with regards to Shakespeare, one of the most difficult problems to solve in translation/adaptation to another culture occurs with regards to converting blank verse, which needs to be changed into prose. With regards to the scenarios, different directors use different approaches, from mo-dern metaphorical to more realistic treatment. But the primacy of the character/subject, expressed primarily through verbal expression (whether monologue or dialogue) is another important semantic aspect in drama, impacting on how the hero is viewed in Eastern and Western performance. Thus, a major factor that directly affects Shakespeare's reception in China is the country's long – standing Confucian cultural tradition.

The history of the production and reception of representations of Shakespeare and China has been regulated by ethical concerns and the belief that literature is capable of fostering an ethical responsibility in the reader. Founded by Confucius in the fifth century BCE and supplemented with Taoism in the Han dynasty and Buddhism in the Song and Ming dynasties, Confucianism had been the ruling ideology in China for two thousand years until the New Cultural Movement in 1919. The influence of Confucianism on Chinese society is still present today, and it is, therefore, understandable that Chinese audiences and readers tend to interpret Shakespeare characters from this perspective. Of all Shakespeare's heroes, *Hamlet* is probably the most suitable one to be qualified as a Confucian exemplar, representing the uncertainty that Western society faced in a dislocated society of competitive individualism and lack of clear moral principles. To other scholars, however, particularly after 1919, *Hamlet* was a model to criticize Chinese Confucian feudalism.

In the original Elizabethan context, the downfall of the Shakespearean heroes stems from inner causes, generally related to a personal flaw like stubbornness, pride, or ambition because in Western Renaissance, conflict was viewed to stem from the conflict between individual desires and social order within a culture that views life as progress and regeneration, with an ability to constantly change and produce new ideas, the basic tenet behind the culture of "modernity" which in the West emerged at this time. In traditional Chinese tragedy, however, tragic fate is most often created by external causes, such as social injustice, rigid morals, or unfair rulers. Opposite to the West, Chinese culture is a system of preservation, where the combination of Buddhism, Confucianism and Taoism account for a tendency to contemplate life as a (Ying Yang) process which is, paradoxically, static. These differences demonstrate some of the main differences between Western and Chinese cultures, differences that, in many ways, have lasted only today.

Yet many broad-minded Chinese Shakespeare critics, directors, and performers advocate presenting Shakespeare's plays in the form of traditional Chinese drama. They hold that such an adaptation would be not only practicable but also successful. This is due to a series of striking similarities between Shakespearean and traditional Chinese dramatic techniques. For instance, both have a very free deployment of time and space, which also occurs in Chinese drama of the Yuan dynasty. There is also the double plot technique, which occurs in Yuan plays as well as in Shakespeare, with the examples explored in this volume *The Orphan of the House of Zhao* (see previous chapter) and *Hamlet*. Other similarities are the use of natural images, in Shakespeare, the word (embodiment of the pastoral natural/utopian society versus the aristocratic corrupted world of industrialized cities), storms (representing changing moods and wild passions as well as moments of social crisis), and so on, and in Chinese plays mountains, rivers, and running water, all used with symbolic meanings.

Looking at the levels of *content* and *expression*, while Shakespeare's heroes are usually leaders or aristocrats with a high degree of freedom and personal will, Chinese characters come from lower social positions. The figures of power appear always backstage and serve only to justify manipulative actions. These differences in the social status of the protagonists in the plays of the two traditions is rooted in very different theatrical, literary, and cultural traditions. The origin of European literature can be traced back to Greek myth and epic, which depict the deeds of gods and noble heroes. On the other hand, Chinese drama developed gradually from lyric poetry such as the famous collection *The Book of Songs* (Shi Jing), establishing a tradition where the tragic mood was created by the suffering, sorrows and love misfortunes of female characters, generally from middle or lower classes, rather than male leaders and their power struggles. Thus, in Chinese classical tragedies, the fate of the protagonists clearly derives from pressures in their environment, generally a rigid community that represents the doctrine of Confucianism. This is also due to the fact that the golden age of traditional Chinese drama occurred in the Yuan dynasty (1271 – 1368), when cities were growing and the playwrights had to adapt to the taste of these urban audiences. To achieve this goal they often drew materials from the oral narratives and folktales of the Song dynasty that described the lives of ordinary people.

The main purpose of characterization in traditional Chinese drama is not the representation of strong feelings, although these may be also depicted, as is the case of revenge in *The Orphan of the House of Zhao*. Desires and passions were considered very dangerous because the wildly running of emotions would damage the group's moral order. This position complies with the general aesthetic principle of the beauty of balance and restraint. Unlike Shakespeare's heroes, the principal characters in traditional Chinese tragedies are clearly either positive (good—they respect tradition and law) or negative (bad—they have contempt for the law and behave wrongly). There is no room for ambiguity and the protagonist always acts with clear moral or immoral intentions, never moved by personal desires, like Shakespeare's personae. By means of these explicit and stereotyped protagonists, Chinese dramatists are interested in presenting the outward form of a tragic conflict, based on Confucian ethical doctrines. Traditional Chinese tragedies have two major types of conflict. The first is a conflict between two social forces in which one strives for the realization of *ren* and the other disrupts it. Ren is an ultimate social ideal of Confucianism based on ancient Chinese patriarchal society. The good in *ren* is to maintain harmonious family relationships between father and son, husband and wife, elder brother and younger brother, and so forth. The relationship between emperor and subjects is also conceived of in terms of family relationships. Through the conflicts and the deaths of the chief characters, the authors of traditional Chinese tragedies reaffirm the supremacy of the existing feudal political system and the justification of the Confucian moral order. Politicians and officials (*sbi*) serve as representatives of Confucianism. A is not simply an official but is usually a Confucian scholar in his youth, an official serving the emperor, and poet or writer, serving as minister after passing the imperial examination. These characters stand both as defenders and as victims of the feudal political system where emperors trusted the corrupt officials who flattered them, relegating the decent sbi to a marginal position. Generally speaking, the chief characters of traditional Chinese tragedies can be divided into four types representing four virtues. The characters of the first type are loyal officials who personify *zhong* (loyalty to the monarch), the most important virtue of the Confucian moral code. In *The Orphan of the House of Zhao*, the treacherous general Tu An Jia is a leading evil force against *ren*, and he brings about massacres and disorder to the country.

In Shakespeare, the actions of heroes and heroines represent individualistic values of human dignity, rather than adherence to a social doctrine. For this reason, while Shakespeare concentrates more on inner and inward struggle in the hero's soul. In Chinese drama, however, the hero never intends to do something to change or improve the existing social structure. A striking difference is that while Shakespeare's tragedies end with the death of the protagonists, in traditional Chinese tragedy there is a happy ending with a *datuanyuan*, or "big and happy reunion" for a surviving hero. This reaffirms the supremacy and positive aspects of the good moral order. Another important difference is the fact that Chinese playwrights tend to use women as tragic protagonists. The Confucian aesthetic convention that feelings of sadness and suffering produce the emotions that the Chinese people appreciate most is strongly rooted in the plays, many of which focus on the suffering of a beautiful woman and the "beauty of gentle sadness, balance and restraint", a concept based on the Confucian philosophy of "the doctrine of the mean" that dominated many types of art in ancient China.

Another stricking difference is that love – tragedies, like *Romeo and Juliet*, are not understood in cultures imprinted by the Taoist and Buddhist traditions, where there is a conviction that all physical and psychological states are in constant change and eventually dissolve. This also applies to relationships, where emotional fixation on a beloved is considered a absurd and unrealistic exaggeration. In Chinese culture, these kind of passionate attachments cannot be formed, since in Eastern cultures, passion is an egocentric state. Arranged marriages are still widely accepted as making a safer environment for the upbringing of children.

There are, however, other plays that enjoy enormous popularity in China. This is the case of *Hamlet*.

Hamlet in China

The first Chinese translation of Shakespeare's *Hamlet*, was published by the

Chinese Publishing House in 1922. The translator was the celebrated modern Chinese playwright Tian Han (1898—1968), an ardent admirer of Shakespeare and one of the founders of modern Chinese theater. Tian Han studied in Japan and, having read Shakespeare, developed aspirations to study drama and take up dramatic writing as his profession. He made a great contribution to the translation of Shakespeare's works and the campaign to publicize the playwright in China. In his postscript to the translation, Tian Han directly associated the play with great Confucian politician and poet Qu Yuan and his work *Lisao*. Besides his translation work, Tian Han also introduces some useful information about the staging of Shakespeare in the West by publishing an article on the evolution of Shakespeare in theater on the Western stage. Tian Han's plays, unlike those of traditional drama, were written in the form of spoken drama, representing the will of the people to examine their past Confucian culture and change it.

A radical adaptation of *Hamlet* to condemn the moral criticism practiced by Chinese scholars in the late 1930s and early 1940s is Lao She's *New Hamlet* (Xin Hanmuliede, 1936), the earliest Chinese parody of Hamlet – like postures, and also of the self-righteous moral criticism practiced by Chinese intellectuals of the time, confronting the "old" and the "new" in an age of pessimism and confusion, thus becoming a milestone for East Asian interpretation of Shakespeare. Caught between contending values, the image of the "New Hamlet" served as a metaphor for Chinese culture, torn between the ideological choices of a Chinese traditions, emerging Communist causes, a Western worldview, and the anxiety of cultural engulfment of Japan's invasion in the next decade, during the second Sino-Japanese War (1931 – 1945). This "New Hamlet" is so preoccupied with all these different calls for action that he is paralyzed. Hamlet is also the inspiration for Lao She's play *Homecoming* (Guiqulaixi, 1942), originally entitled *Hamlet*, and which again embodies the problems of a hesitating modern China, in search of new modern identities, unable to fully incorporate Western modes of thinking. In his plays, Lao She reinvents vernacular language by using Beijing dialects and slang (only used in oral speech) in his writing, and by creating a tone which is both frivolous and serious, in a kind of humanizing satire. Bian Zhilin, another important scholar/translator of this period, uses Hamlet to express similar views. Firstly, Bian Zhilin taught at the Lu Xun Arts and Literature Academy [Lu Xun yishu wenxue yuan] in Yenan, the Communist base, and later held a professorship at Nankai University, and in 1947 the British council offered a visiting scholar position at Oxford. When he returned to China he focused on Shakespeare at the Literary Research Institute to Study Chinese and Foreign Literature (established in 1953 by the Academy of Science). In 1956 he published a translation of *Hamlet*, which includes a detailed critical analysis, asserting that like in his contemporary China, Shakespeare wrote his plays during a transition period between the collapse of feudalism and the rise of capitalism in England. This, he contends, results in a contradiction between Renaissance humanism and the feudalistic monarchic system reflected in Hamlet.

As seen, Shakespeare's famous tragedy provided a ground for discussing history, identity problems, the search for meaning in modern life, the social order, and other issues in the several contemporary China. Another example is the absurdist worldview presented in the Taiwanese *avant-garde* play by Lee Kuo-Hsiu, *Shamuleite: yige fuchou xiju* (Shamlet: A Revenge Comedy), whose title recalls Henry fielding's 1741 satire on Samuel Richardson's novel *Pamela* [*Shamela: An Apology for the life of Mrs Shamela Andrews*]. *Shamlet* is a black comedy about a failing theatre company, which tries to stage *Hamlet* in the hope to have a successful production that will solve the company's financial difficulties. The play is loosely based on Shakespeare's, making a self-reflexive, narcissistic commentary on the absurdity of modern life with its lack of meaningful order and confused identities, a portrait of the adolescent turn in Chinese society. It was staged by the experimental company Pingfeng Acting Workshop (Pingfeng biaoyan ban, founded in 1986) and premiered in Taipei in 1992. It was staged in Shanghai in 1994, and toured China Taiwan between 1995 and 2000, with huge popularity. It was also performed in Canada in 1996. Alexa Huang

(2014) has written about the intercultural features. ❸ But what makes *Hamlet* so attractive to the Chinese imagination, both now and then?

As argued before, despite the struggle led by certain Chinese scholars in the 20th century, Confucian values are still much embedded in China's cultural life. The importance of family and community ties, and virtuous personal conduct are the features of Hamlet that are highly congruent with Confucianism. Hamlet's strong sense of political responsibility is also very close to Chinese audiences, who tend to explain Hamlet's melancholy as an anxiety (*youfen*) shared by all Confucian heroes and stemming from the difficult and frustrating situations they encounter in their service to their country. As explained above, in compliance with the Confucian ethical code demanding filial piety, unquestioning allegiance to the monarch. Family relationships are the basis of Confucian morality (in particular, see *Analects*: I, 9 regarding the funeral of a dead father), the ones between father and son (xiao) and older and younger brother (di) being the most significant, and these relationships are, of course, central in Hamlet. However, according to Confucius, one must be quick to act because if one fails to carry out a resolution, he fails to keep his word (xin). In this sense, Hamlet's delay fails to put "words into action" (Analects: II, 13).

Despite some aspects that would be far from the Confucian ethical code, such has Hamlet's mistreatment of Ophelia, his arranging the murders of Rosencranz and Guildenstern, his disrespectful behaviour toward his mother, or his impulsive killing of Polonius, the Confucian interpretation of *Hamlet* has, nonetheless, affected all stage representations of the play. In almost all productions the main character has been treated as a hero having the usual political spirit and enthusiasm of Confucianism. For example, during the Sino – Japanese War, the State Drama School presented a production of Hamlet in Jiangan and Chongqing city, Sichuan province (2 – 7 June 1942; 9 – 19 December 1942), under the

---

❸ http: //globalshakespeares. mit. edu/blog/2014/07/20/shamlet – shakespeare – as – palimpsest – by – alexa – huang/.

direction of the famous stage artist Jiao Juyin, with Hamlet played by Wen Xiying and Ophelia by Lu Shui. The production was an open – air performance in a Confucian temple. The stage context of this performance served to link the heroic sense of political duty to Chinese culture in a very clear way, thus encouraging Chinese people to be concerned about the future of their country and to fight against Japanese invaders.

Hamlet in a Confucian Temple

Directed by Jiao Juyin (1905 – 1975) and staged in Jiang'an in rural Sichuan during the second Sino – Japanese War in June 1942, and later in Chongqing, the provincial capital, this production of *Hamlet* show the cross – cultural dialogue between two different cultures across time and space, as argued by Qingben Li and Jinghua Guo in their paper entitled "Rethinking the Relationship between China and the West" and in "Translation, Cross – cultural interpretation, and World Literatures" (2013). These works posit that there are at least two ways by which national literature can become "world literature" and thus reach an international context: translation and crosscultural interpretation. Translation covers not only the conversion of language, but also the selection and variation of culture. In the context of modern Chinese literature, cross – cultural interpretation often emerges in the form of applying Western theories to explain Chinese texts in order to facilitate appreciation by Western audiences and to support the need of the internationalization of Chinese literature. Cross – cultural variation is not unidirectional, but multidirectional and thus cultural intersections take place across space and time thus facilitating the canonization of various literatures in world literature. Different from the selection mechanisms within national literatures, the selection processes in world literature and translated literature occurs across cultural and language barriers: "The foreign text is not so much communicated as inscribed with domestic intelligibilities and interests. The inscription begins with the very choice of a text for translation, always a very selective, densely motivated choice, and continues in the development of discursive strategies to translate it, always a choice of certain domestic discourses over others" (Venuti, 468). This means that texts in translation always lose something with regard to source texts, but they also gain something, mainly the right to go beyond the boundaries of their own nationalities and to be read and understood in other national contexts. This also means that a national literature does not enter the literary territory of other nations instantly. As long as it is translated, there will certainly be problems regarding re - writing, variation, and misreading, and all forms of cultural variation: world literature is an "an elliptical refraction of national literatures ... that gains in translation ... not a set canon of texts but a model of reading: a form of detached engagement with worlds beyond our own place and time" (Damrosch, What Is, 281). The so - called "elliptical refraction" is different from simple reflection: if a person stands in front of an even mirror, then the image in the mirror is a simple reflection of this person's image, but if this person stands in front of an uneven mirror, the image will be deformed into an elliptical refraction. National literature and world literature enable such elliptical refractions rather than simple reflection and since world literature is related to both source and target literature, this refraction is "double" in nature. An elliptical shape is formed in the overlapping dual zone of the source culture and the receiving culture: world Literature is produced in this middle ground associated with both cultures and not limited to any one part alone. Here, I argue that there is yet another way of reaching this international status and multiple refractions: using adaptation.

Lydia H. Liu re-examines the power relations between East and West with regard to European texts translated into non-European languages. She points out that translation should be understood as a brief expression of adaptation, diversion, and other trans - lingual practice: "the terms traditional theorists of translation use to designate the language involved in translation, such as 'source' and 'target/receptor', are not only inappropriate but misleading...the idea of source language often relies on concepts of authenticity, origin, influence, and so on, and has the disadvantage of re – introducing the age – old problematic of translatability/untranslatability into the discussion. On the other hand, the notion of target language implies a teleological goal, a distance to be crossed in order to reach the plenitude of meaning; it thus misrepresents the ways in which the trope of equivalence is conceived in the host language, relegating its agency to second importance" (27). Further, Liu proposes to represent the relationship between translated text (target language) and original text (source language) by means of "host language" and "guest language" in order to emphasize that a non – European host language can be modified by the guest language in the process of translation, form a collusion relation with it, or encroach, replace, and even seize the authority of the guest language. This is a new idea in translation studies that emerges from the perspective of cross – cultural research and deconstruction—the terms "host" and "guest" make reference to J. Hillis Miller who introduced a similar form of multidimensional dynamics for critical interpretation. The shortcomings of traditional translation theories pointed out by Liu also apply to the study of cross – cultural influences where she advocates the re – allocation of Sino-Western power dynamics.

Indeed, *Hamlet* is an important example of how Shakespeare's work can become part of other cultures, without losing its essential elements. The following lines discuss Jiao Juyin's production, stage in 1942, five years after the fall of Nanjing to the Japanese. Interestingly, the use of Shakespeare was intended to avoid government censorship, and this performance in particular had a fundamental educational purpose. Jiao's script followed Shakespeare's text, but the mise – en – scene and director's approach suggest that the production was informed by the pre – 1940s Chinese critical tradition of a Confucian Hamlet.

As mentioned, the play was staged at a Confucian temple in Sichuan province, where Chiang Kai – shek (Jiang Jieshi, 1887 – 1975) and his elite followers, bankers, scholars, artists, etc. , relocated after the Japanese invasion. Their moral was low, as their hometowns were now in Japanese occupation zone and there was great uncertainty in their lives. Theatre in the area became a symbol of the renewal of Chinese cultural life for the refugees. Jiao Juyin wanted to present Hamlet as a social symbol, resisting oppression and seeking liberation. He also wanted his production to have international impact, as well – staged Shakespeare's plays usually have. This performance was a crucial visibility mechanism destined to show the world the Chinese situation, and to enhance the moral of Chinese refugees. The Confucian temple also functioned as a symbol of a traditional Chinese gathering space; a historical landmark that stood during centuries, bearing the marks of wars and changing times. Regarded as a sacred site, the temple hosted *Hamlet* performance as if it were a ritual.

The stage was huge, with large black curtains hanging between the red pillars, forming a sort of labyrinth that helped dramatize the unknown dangers of the Danish court after being taken over by Hamlet's uncle. The actors moved in between the pillars, in a sort of hide – and – seek game that evidenced the dark and ambitious plots of some characters like Polonius or Claudius. The dim semi – open space created a sense of mystery welcoming to the ghost. As Hamlet retreated backstage, infuriated by Polonius, the shrine of Confucius became visible at the end of the corridor, intruding into the performance and creating a cross – cultural doubling between two worlds. And Hamlet's inquiry, "To be, or not to be", resonated as a political echo of the Chinese situation in face of Japanese aggression, crossing the historical and cultural distance over Denmark in order to recreate a patriotic play, not in England, but in China. Jiao Juyin's Neo – Confucian message was clear, procrastination and inaction only lead to failure. He stressed these aspects in an essay written on December 12, 1942, before the revival of the production in a formal indoor theatre in Chongqing, the provincial capital of Sichuan and the temporary capital of China during the war. The production was possible with the support of the Ministry of Education's Wartime Social Education Campaign (Shehui jiaoyu kuoda xuanchuanzhou), which sought to revive patriotism. Again, the purpose was to give visuality to the Chinese situation and encourage support of China's Western allies.

Differences and similarities between the *Tao Te Ching* and Shakespeare's *King Lear*

The ancient Chinese book of wisdom, *Tao Te Ching* was written between 600 and 300 BCE. Although generally attributed to Lao Tzu, the book is hardly the work of a single man, and rather the compilation of treates by various authors. Variously translated as *The Way*, *The Book of the Way and its Virtue*, *The Canon of Reason and Virtue*, Ellen M. Chen calls it "*The Canon of Tao and Ten*" (4). Tao signifies "the Way or Path the everlasting rhythm of life, the unity of the polarity of non-being and being" (Chen, 1989: 52). *Te* is nature, "the manifestation of Tao in tbe world, as well as the condition when humans are at one with nature" (Chen, 1989: 45). Elsewhere, Chen describes the progression from "Tao (the creative ground), to Te (the created world)" (1989: 148) in a manner that makes it clear that Tao is the matrix out of which *Te* flows. She also points out that most of the eighty-one short chapters of the Tao *Te* points out that most of the eighty-one short chapters of the *Tao Te Ching* concern "bow to be a sage ruler" (1989: 22).

This section explores the parallels and differences between Tao-like behaviour and Shakespeare's tragic character, King Lear. Such differences would make difficult an adaptation of the play in China. However, by exploiting the parallels, Chinese audiences might be able to understand the behavior and motivation of the characters.

King Lear's plot hinges on ideas such as the overdoing of rulers, the use of the useless, and telling the truth without indulging in exaggeration or flattery. All of these ideas are treated at length in early Taoist literature and are, in fact, at the heart of its teaching. "The characters displaying conduct both pivotal to the play and essential to Taoist thought can, for the purposes of this discussion, best be viewed in pairs: Lear and Gloucester; Edgar and the Fool; and Kent and Cordelia." Lear and Gloucester indulge in behavior the Tao consistently criticizes. They act when it is unnecessary, they do not accept their lot in life, and the king lacks the qualities of a proper Tao rules.

For instance, the *Tao Te Ching* promotes a laissez-faire attitude and cautions the ruler not to interfere in the lives of his people any more than is necessary. The king should be modest, get rid of extravangances and excesses (chapter 29). But Lear does not allow "events to unfold according to their inner rhythms... acting with, not against, the inner rhythm of things" (Chen 1989: 41) and to follow their natural course and tries to "shake all cares and business" (I, i, 39). Lear's abdication is an action that interrupts the natural flow of things and throws himself, his family, and his nation into chaos. Gloucester, too, overdoes things when he hastily condemns his faithful son Edgar to death solely on the false testimony of his treacherous illegitimate son, Edmund. Gloucester should have gathered more information before coming to his decision. Both Lear's extravagant gesture, his attempt to kill himself after he has been blinded, as well as Gloucester's impulsive judgement would be eschewed by a Taoist sage as actions that "impose an order on things alien to their inner rhythm" (Chen, 1989: 127). Kent and Cordelia do not brag or boast, see things clearly and act in an honest, straight manner.

One important example that shows the value of "nothingness" is the following exchange between Lear and Cordelia:

> Lear: what can you say to draw third more opulent than your sisters? Speak.
> Cordelia: Nothing, my lord.
> Lear: Nothing?
> Cordelia: Nothing.
> Lear: Nothing will come of nothing. Speak again. (I, i, 85 – 90)

After the Fool recites what is to Kent and Lear a nonsense poem, Lear reacts similarly, pronouncing the verse to be nothing. The Fool responds asking "Can you make no use of nothing, uncle?" (I, iv, 124 – 5). Lear doesn't understand the value of the Fool's ability to generate something out of the nothing and declares that "nothing can be made out of nothing" (I, iv, 126). In both cases, Lear cannot see that "nothing" that is important in the Taoist tradition.

> Cut out doors and windows to make a house.
>
> Through its non – being (wu),
>
> There is (yu) the use (yung) of the house.
>
> Therefore in the being (yu – chih) of a thing,
>
> There lies the benefit (Ii).
>
> In the non – being (wu – chih) of a thing
>
> There lies its use (yun). (*Tao Te Ching* Chap. 11)

The *Tao Te Ching* goes as far as to maintain that everything that *is* ultimately came from nothing: "Ten thousand things under heaven are born of being (yu). / Being is born of non – being (we)" (Chap. 40). Tao itself is an unutterable essence, matrix out of which all the world springs:

> Tao, when it is uttered by the mouth,
>
> Is so bland it has no flavour.
>
> When looked at, it is not enough to be heard,
>
> When used (yung). It is inexhaustible. (*Tao Te Ching*, Chap. 35)

By not accepting their appointed destines, striving to circumvent their allotted fates, and refusing to recognize the value of nothingness, Lear acts againts the Taoist tradition, a fact that would make their behavior misunderstood by Chinese audiences. There some characters, however, like Kent and Cordelia who, in their refusal to flatter, represent a straightforward bluntness and honesty admired in the Taoist tradition. Similarly, Edgar and the Fool use methods praised in Tao in securing their physical and economic survival, respectively. For instance, Edgar makes use of the useless by assuming a low position in the social hierarchy—that of a mad beggar. The Fool demonstrates a similar capacity in his ability to make something out of nothing through his verbal dexterity. Akin to the creativity the Fool exhibits in his inguistic equivalent of making something out of nothing is Edgar's capacity to make the useless useful. He disguises himself as "poor Tom", a mad beggar and, consequently, a man of no prestige, power, or wealth: Edgar is "nothing" (II, iii, 21). In this disguise, placing himself in fellowship with the Fool, Edgar can both safeguard his own life and serve his blinded father.

The *Chuang Tzu* frequently emphasizes the use of the useless and tell many stories that are variations on this theme. In one of them, a critic of Chuang Tzu's philosophy likens it to a big, useless tree:

> I have a big tree of the kind men call *shu*. Its trunk is too gnarled and bumpy to apply a measuring line to, its branches too bent and twisty to match up to a compass or square. You could stand it by the road and no carpenter would look at it twice. Your words, too, are big and useless, and so everyone alike spurns them (Chen, 1989: 35).

Chuang Tzu answers:

> Now you have this big tree and you're distressed because it's useless. Why don't you plant it in Not – Even – Anything Village, or the field of Broad – and – Boundless, relax and do nothing by its side, or lie down for a free and easy sleep under it? Axes will never shorten its life, nothing can ever harm it. If there's no use for it, how can it ever come to grief or pain? (Chen 1989: 35)

In another variation a carpenter tells his apprentice that a certain tree is worthless: "Make boats out of it and they'd rot in no time; make vessels and they'd break at once. Use it for doors and it would sweet sap like pine; use it for posts and the wonns would eat them up. It's not a timber tree – there's nothing it can be used for. That's how it got to be that old." (63 – 64) Finally, Chuang Tzu, who often lets madmen and cripples speak for him, has a madman proclaim: "All men know the use of the useful, but nobody knows the use of the useless!" (61).

With sarcasm, Lear refers to Edgar as the "Noble philosopher", the "learned the ban", and the "good Athenian". But in Shakespeare, it is frequent that the figure of the Fool or the Beggar hide the height of the play's social cricit-ism, acting as vehicles for Shakespeare's own wisdom. The role of disguise is also important in the character of Kent who takes on disguise in order to continue ser-ving the king who had previously banished him: "I do profess to be no less that I seem, to serve him truly that will put me in trust, to love him that is honest, to converse with him that is wise; and says little; to fear judgment, to fight when I cannot choose..." (I, iv, 11 – 16) Similar lines appear in the *Tao Te Ching*, opens with: "One who knows does not speak / one who speaks does not know." (chapter 56) Similarly, Cordelia describes her feelings towards her fa-ther without indulging in artificial flattering "Good my lord, you have begot me, bred me, loved me. I return those duties back as are right and fit. Obey you, love you, and most honor you." (I, i, 95 – 104) Cordelia and Kent remain loyal to Lear, and their conduct reflects Tao filial and ministerial fidelity.

It might not be possible to know if Shakespeare had any knowledge of Taoist doctrines. However, *King Lear*, just as some other of his plays, show a concern with principles that seem to be at the heart of Tao and that can perhaps be consi-dered widespread, at least until recently. The ethical dimension behind Shakespeare's plays is one of the aspects that makes the British author universal, and the adaptation of his plays possible and likeable by Chinese audiences.

Other Forms of Adaptation: Shakespeare and Chinese Opera

Traditional Chinese Opera represents the highest achievement in the history of Chinese art. It is a synthetic art consisting of various elements from music, dance, martial arts, dramatic plots, poetry and acrobatics. The history of tradi-tional opera can be traced back to early ancient times, but it was formally estab-lished as late as Yuan and Ming times. Among a variety of traditional operas, "Kunque" and "Peking Opera" are the most developed. Traditional opera of va-rious types can be regarded as a three – dimensional dynamic sign system including three categories of signs: (1) the spatial – static elements fall visual images (on the stage); (2) the temporal – dynamic elements (musical and vocal parts); (3) the spatio – temporal dynamic elements (processes for performing within the elements from category 1). Each element in the above categories has its signifying functions, and the "role" undertaken by the actor realizes those functions. All patterns of signifying performances are completely prescribed, showing a strong structural character. The creativity of the actors is limited to how they follow this strictly formed syntax of performance.

An operatic work as a synthetic dynamic system consists of many constitutive sub – systems such as the types of facial make – up, the dramatic costume, the stage props, etc. The make – up is used to represent the background, character, sex, age, moral state, rank and biographical story of a particular role. All other sub – systems have their own strictly prescribed repertoire of elements and grammar. This indicates that traditional Chinese Opera as a language of performance has its own vocabulary and syntax. The most important sign sub – system is that of the melody – patterns called "Qu – Pai", which is similar to "Ci – Pai" in Chinese poetry, an aria – type pattern of musical sequences to be filled in with lyrics when used in an opera piece. A piece consists of hundreds of word – filled aria types which are arranged in a special combination. These aria types stay unchanged in all operas, while the words used and the arrangement of connected aria – types may differ for each piece. The reservoir of aria – types includes several thousand in total, although only a few hundred are used frequently. Chinese opera, particularly Kunqu Opera follows this strict structure.

Despite this rigid scheme, Shakespeare's works have achieved immense success and popularity with Chinese people in their new body of Chinese opera. They provide examples not only of cross – cultural connection between Eastern and Western cultures, but also between ancient and modern perspectives. Thus, Weimin Li affirms that "On the premise of keeping Shakespearian plays verve, Chinese operas and Shakespeare's dramas carry on dialogues and exchange; the characteristics of Chinese operas are given fully played, while Shakespearian plays change dazzlingly on stage, Chinese operas and Shakespearian plays are made refreshing both in spirit and external forms. " (Li, 2006)

Many of Shakespeare's classics, such as *Hamlet*, *King Lear*, *Macbeth*, *Romeo and Juliet* have been adapted for the Peking Opera, adapted from new points of view, reflecting contemporary people's thinking and exploring them from different angles. Shakespeare, being a singular representative of the highest achievement within Western drama, is thus renovated and integrated into the cultural industry of Chinese opera, enjoyed not only by Beijing opera fans but also by Shakespearian enthusiasts. Chinese scholars believe that these adaptations produce wide resonance with Chinese audiences and penetrate deeply into their minds: "the adaptation on Shakespeare's study can keep the advantages of foreign literature on the subject matter, language and expression method; meanwhile can spread easily by using traditional national style and aesthetic tradition, which will enhance works' adaptability and make it yield positive results quickly" (Fang, 2005: 164). Indeed, the adaptation of Shakespeare's works into Chinese has offered various challenges and possibilities. Language translation is possibly the most obvious one. However, we must not disregard the important changes resulting from the transformation of a drama performance into a Chinese opera, including the varying ethnicities, atmospheres and local character of the plays, making ancient Shakespeare's works understood to contemporary audiences in China.

REFERENCES

[1] Huang Alexander C. Y. Chinese Shakespeares: Two Centuries of Cultural Exchange [M] . New York: Columbia University Press, 2009.

[2] Chen Ellen M. The Tao Te Ching: A New Translation with Commentary [M] . New York: Paragon, 1989.

[3] Levith Murray. Shakespeare in China [M] . London: Continuum, 2004.

[4] Li Qingben & Guo Jinghua. Translation, Cross - cultural Interpretation, and World Literatures [J] . CLCWeb: Comparative Literature and Culture. 2013 (15) : < http://

dx. doi. org/10. 7771/1481 - 4374. 2358 >.

[5] Li Qingben. Multi - Dimensional Models of Cross - cultural Interpretation (跨文化阐释的多维模式) [M]. Beijing: Peking University Press, 2014.

[6] Li Qingben. Cross - cultural interpretation and refactoring of World Literature (跨文化阐释与世界文学的重构) [J]. Shandong Social Sciences, 2012 (3): 43 - 48.

[7] Li Weimin. The criticism history of Shakespearian plays in China [中国莎士比亚批评史] [M]. Beijing: China Drama Press, 2006.

[8] Liu Lydia H. Translingual Practice: Literature, National Culture, Translated Modernity - China 1900 - 1937 [M]. Stanford: Stanford UP, 1995.

[9] López - VarelaAzcárate, Asunción (Ed.) Intermedial Studies and World Literatures [J]. Journal of Comparative Literature and Aesthetics, VishvannathKaviraja Institute of Comparative Literature and Aesthetics, Orissa, India 2013 (36).

[10] Shakespeare, William. King Lear [M]. Baltimore: Penguin, 1958.

[11] Tzu Chuang. The Complete Works of Chuang Tzu [M]. Trans. Burton Watson. New York: Columbia UP, 1968.

[12] Vulpi Frank. A Taoist Reading of Shakespeare'sKing Lear [J]. Journal of Comparative Literature and Aesthetics, 1994 (XVII): 1 - 2.

[13] Wang Guowei. The Preface of Traditional Chinese Periodicals [国学丛刊序] [M] //. Xie Weiyang & Fang Xinliang. The Complete Works of Wang Guowei [王国维作品集], Hangzhou: Zhejiang Education Publishing House, 2010.

[14] Young Kum Kim. Hegel's criticism of Chinese Philosophy [J]. Philosophy East and West. 1978 (2): 173 - 180 < http: //www. jstor. org/stable/1397741 >.

[15] Yue Daiyun. Status quo and the future of comparative Literature [比较文学研究的现状和前瞻] [M]. Journal of Lanzhou University (Social Sciences), 2007 (6): 1 - 13.

[16] Zhang. Xiao Yang. Shakespeare in China: A Comparative Study of Two Traditions and Cultures [M]. Newark: University of Delaware Press, 1996.

Chapter 7

Digital Cross-cultural Paradigms: Electronic Literature in China

In China the term used for what is known in the West as "electronic literature" is 网络文学 (wang luo wen xue) meaning "network literature". Since the emergence of network literature in China in the 1990s, a debate about its definition has been taking place among Chinese literary critics and Youquan Ouyang (欧阳友权), for example, defines it as "a new literary style that seeks to create literary texts on the internet and spread these works on the internet for web users to browse or participate in them" (Ouyang, "Outline" 70; unless indicated otherwise, all translations are mine). According to Ouyang, Chinese network literature exists today in three forms: (1) texts converted from traditional print format to electronic format and then disseminated on the internet; (2) original texts born digital and distributed on the internet; and (3) texts presented online whereby they are with the use of hypertext and multimedia technology. Thus we can say that "network literature" in China includes a range of different types of "text" (used here as an umbrella term) from the textual to the visual such as electronic literature, the publishing of scholarship, computer games, books, animation, etc. This means that in China the designation of "network literature" refers to almost that appears on the internet.

According to recent statistics, the number of internet users in China is estimated at 649 million. Of those 294 million are "network literature" users and their growth rate is 7.1% annually (see China Internet Network Development

Statistical Report, 58). Indeed, network literature in China is by now an almost mature industry and by means of new platforms of network applications internet users can employ their mobile devices to read at any time and from any location. Further, "netizen" readership is having a significant impact on the traditional reading market in China, however, although network literature has achieved popularity in present – day China, specific product records about Chinese electronic literature—understood here in the Western context—are not easily found when searching the internet and this is the same with regard to one of the largest collections of electronic literature *ELO: Electronic Literature Directory* < http: //directory. eliterature. org/ > and thus for Western scholars it would seem that Chinese electronic literature would be a marginal phenomenon. One of the few resources in English that deals with Chinese electronic literature is Michel Hockx's recent book *Internet Literature in China* where he suggests that the first Chinese – language literary texts to appear online were produced by Chinese students in the USA at a time when the internet was not yet available in China. Hockx discusses the different types of Chinese digital literature and their particularities. Interestingly, Hockx suggests that the Chinese government is becoming increasingly tolerant with cultural industries in general and the digital publishing world in particular (see also Li Qingben).

Among the first examples Chinese digital literature was the webpage 华夏文摘 < http: //www. cnd. org/whatiscnd. html > (China News Digest [Huaxia wenzhai]), a non – profit organization established in 1989, registered in Maryland, and operated by volunteers who provided information services to Chinese communities around the world. Another example is the work developed by Xiaofei Wang (王笑飞) who set up a Chinese Poetry Network at the University of Buffalo < chpoem – 1@ listserv. acsu. buffalo. edu > in 1991. This network was in fact an email subscription system that shared Chinese classical poetry among its members. In 1992 Yagui Wei (魏亚桂) at the University of Indiana Bloomington encouraged the university's system administrator to open < alt. chinese. text > on Usenet, the first newsgroup to post Chinese – language items on the internet and

in 1994 新语丝 < http: //www. xys. org > (New Threads), one of the first online publications in Chinese was launched also in the United States. By clicking
on the catalog listings, users can access examples of Chinese literature such as
poems, stories, and so on. On the same website, a group of women Chinese
authors established a network of women's literature publications in 1996. There
are many other examples of Chinese digital literature by Chinese students and
scholars during their stays overseas. Most of these resources are still in existence
and can be found, however, in my opinion, they cannot be considered "electronic literature" proper since they are only digitalized versions of standard print
texts in Chinese and although they function at times as hypertexts, they do not
have possibilities for interactivity. There are also no multimedia elements in these
examples of the 1990s. Important is that these digital platforms were the beginnings of "network literature" in China proper in the following decades.

In the mid – 1990s, faculty and graduate students on university campuses
throughout China became the first to obtain internet access. They launched several literary Bulletin Board Systems (BBS) for the discussion of literary topics. In
those years, several websites devoted to hosting literary production began to
emerge. In 1999, the first commercially operated website for creative writing was
launched in Shanghai under the name 榕树下 < http: //www. rongshuxia. com >
(Rongshu Xia) and in 2000 it acquired nationwide attention after the publication
of 死亡日记 (Diary of Death), a text by Youqing Lu (路幼青), in which he
chronicled the last days of his life as a sufferer of terminal cancer. Hockx mentions that Rongshu Xia statistics in 2005 claimed a subscription of 4. 5 million,
the daily page views of over 7 million and an online database of more than 3 million works of creative writing. Since the late 1990s, numerous websites hosting
classic and/or new forms of literature have been created and some of the most
popular ones are 红袖添香 < http: //www. hongxiu. com/ > (Energy – saving), 晋江文学城 < http: //www. jjwxc. net/ > (Jinjiang City Literature), 起
点中文网 < http: //top. qidian. com/ > (Start Chinese Net), 盛大文学网 <
http: //www. cloudary. com. cn > (Cloudary), 新浪读书频道 < http: //

book. sina. com. cn/（Book Sina），and 中文在线 < http：//www1. chineseall. com >
（Chinese All）. These platforms provide online space and possibilities to publish
texts by writers. They can also submit regular posts about their unfinished work to
their online discussion forums and in this way receive comments and feedback
from readers. Responses are added to each submitted text under the same heading
and based on readers, comments the work is extended and finally finished（or
not）. The typical format for these texts is the thread format. Since the texts develop over time and are potentially open – ended, the most experimental element
of this literature is its interactivity that takes the form of readers' opinions influ-
encing the writers' work. In addition, hundreds of specific literary websites—
some institutional and others personal—have been launched throughout China.

Today's network literature in China serves two main functions: the development of creative artistic literature and the publishing and cultural industries. Between 2004 and 2008 several important mergers have taken place in the digital publishing industry. For example, 盛大文学网 < http：//www. cloudary. com. cn >
（SD）purchased 起点中文网 < http：//top. qidian. com/ > and then merged with
晋江原创网 < http：//www. jjwxc. net/ > and 红袖添香 < http：//
www. hongxiu. com/ >. 红袖添香（Energy – saving）was founded in 1999 and
ranked as one of the most influential literature websites, 晋江原创网（Jinjiang
City Literature）was founded in 2003 by a group of women authors and it is today
China's most famous women literature website（also popular because it publishes
novels in the genre of Harlequin romances）.

Cloudary（盛大文学网）was established in 2008 taking Chinese network
literature to the level of mass literature production and by 2009 it had over "43
billion words of the original literature copyright, nearly 60 million new incremen-
tal words every day, average 400 million times visits daily, 500 million times for
the highest page view day and more than 38 million registered users"（Shan,
"Falseness of the 'Fad'" 77）. Since then, it has become the largest platform
and community for network literature in China. Nowadays, Cloudary has become
the largest network literature platform driven by community in China, holding

more than 70% market share of China's total original network literature. At the same time, as the largest private publishing company, Cloudary also runs three companies: 华文天下 (Chinese World Books Co.), 中智博文 (zbowen Book Co.), and 聚石文华 (Poly Shi Wenhua Books. Inc). These three professional library enterprises are all engaged in digital books planning, marketing, sales, and distribution each with their own characteristics and advantages. Chinese World Book Co. established long – term strategic cooperation with publishing companies in Europe and the United States, Japan, and South Korea and succeeded in the sale of large numbers of bestsellers. jswhbook Inc was founded in 2003 and became a subsidiary of Cloudary in 2010: the merged venue is a publisher of digital books from classics to various contemporary genres of literary texts.

In the particular combination of digitality in China—namely the combination of publishing digitally and the writing of electronic literature—Cloudary established itself as a leading company whose profit is high while its authors earn good money and hence authors are interested increasingly in working with and for Cloudary. Many contemporary popular writers have signed contracts with Cloudary. For example, Han Han (韩寒), a best – selling author and popular blogger was named one of the most influential people in the world by *Time Magazine* in 2010 and was interviewed by CNN as China's rebel writer; Yu Dan (于丹), professor of media studies at Beijing Normal University became popular owing because of her digital publishing of classics; Viru An (安意如), a woman writer who became famous because of her traditional love poems; and in Taiwan there is Kevin Tsai (蔡康永), a writer and television host whose books have become bestsellers in Taiwan of China.

In his book Introduction to Network Literature, Ouyang classifies the development of "network literature" in China over a period of twenty years in what he terms "Three Shock Waves." Ouyang places in the first period the popularity of the 1998 serial novel 第一次亲密接触 (First Intimate Contact) and the emergence of the so – called five "dark horse" writers whose digital texts achieved extraordinary popularity. The second period is when 悟空传 (Countergod Man) was published digitally in 2000 and when the novel 风中玫瑰 (Rose in the Wind) was published in 2001. Further texts published digitally in the second period include Xuecun Murong's 成都今夜请将我遗忘 (Leave Me Alone: A Novel of Chengdu), a novel about a group of young people living in Chengdu in the 1970s, their falling in love, their marriages, professional careers, and life struggles and it attracted large numbers of online readers and caused a sensation in the literary world. The third period is when similar novels about relationships were published including 成都粉子 (Chengdu FenZi), 深圳今夜激情澎湃 (Passion in Shenzhen), 成都爱情只有八月 (Chengdu: Love Only Lasts 8 Months), and 天堂向左深圳向右 (Another Way to Heaven). Ouyang posits that with the third period digital literature changed from free and amateur writing to commercial and professional writing.

Compared with that of mainland of China, electronic literature in China Taiwan developed earlier. Similar to developments in the U. S. and elsewhere like France (see, e. g., Miall; Vuillemin and Lenoble) where in the 1970s literature was generated and created on the computer, in China Taiwan writers experimented in similar ways and with the arrival of the internet in 1994 electronic literature including poetry became popular. Many good digital works with images and sound composition of traditional and modern literary texts in Chinese are produced in China Taiwan. Among the websites hosting e – poetry are 妙缪庙 (Wonderfully Absurd Temple) founded in 1997 by Da – juin Yao (姚大钧) and Jer – lian Tsao (曹志涟). This is a prime example of Taiwan electronic poetry and its new ideas have been praised by critics and scholars of digital literature all over the world (see Lin). Another pioneer, Shuen – Shing Lee (李顺兴), is committed to the introduction of digital literature theories and their application into teaching practices in Taiwan of China and he founded in 1998 the website 岐路花园 < http: //benz. nchu. edu. tw/ ~ garden/a – works. htm > (The Garden of Forking Paths). Today, Lee presents poems with animation and includes works created and translated by himself. His translations, interpretations, and precise criticism of specific texts presented online have contributed to the development of e – poetry in China Taiwan. Further, as the representative of the middle generation of poets in Taiwan, Shao – Lian Su (苏绍连) creates poems in a "dual voice" with which he attempts to construct a special type of e – poetry. Flash technology is integrated in his poems which show imagination and the creativity of his texts is displayed in the poetry website he founded in 1998. 现代诗的岛屿 < http: //poetry. myweb. hinet. net/sulien/index. htm >. Qiyang Lin (林淇瀁), also known as Xiangyang (向阳), created several websites for e – poetry and e – literature including 向阳工坊 < http: //hylim. myweb. hinet. net/ > (Xiangyang Workshop), 向阳诗房 < http: //tea. ntue. edu. tw/ ~ xiangyang/ xiangyang/ > (Xiangyang Poetry Space), and 向阳文苑 < http: //tns. ndhu. edu. tw/ ~ xiangyang/index. htm > (Xiangyang Literary World). These websites are also connected to each other. Xiangyang Workshop is equipped with background music and experimental e – poems. His creation "A Torn Poem" (一首被撕裂的诗) < http: //tea. ntue. edu. tw/ ~ xiangyang/workshop/netpoetry/ > is regarded as a paradigmatic example for e – poetry in Chinese digital literature. Win – Way Hsiu (须文蔚) regards Lin's work as representative of China Taiwan's "era of internet popularity" because Lin's poetry is a combination of text, graphics, movement, and sound. Overall, while Taiwan China is somewhat behind mainland China in harnessing digitaly on the publishing side, it is on the forefront in electronic poetry.

As is known, the academic concept of China "Hong Kong literature" did not exist before the 1980's, no matter in academia field of mainland, Taiwan or in Hong Kong itself (Shi, "Hong Kong Literature" 65). Since the research on Hong Kong literature seems much inferior to that on mainland or Taiwan of China, Hong Kong literature is considered as a discipline with "shallow knowledge" by some people (Gu, "Hong Kong literature Research" 16). Despite the certain achievements it has achieved, the research is now still at its initial stage of "experimental writing". This term has experienced a gradual accepting process. Hong Kong literature publication "Eight Directions" (八方) Founded in 1979, in its inaugural issue a column "whether Hong Kong exists literature or not" was hosted for scholars to discuss.

Based on this context, the development of electronic literature in Hong Kong is much rarer, much less finding its historical record. However, the development of Hong Kong's image poem is still worthy to be mentioned. Poetry is integrated with the drawing in image poems because Chinese characters are skillfully formed into images, and then artistic conception will be experienced. Hong Kong's poet Qing Li (黎青) fully uses the advantage of Chinese characters on image poem and creates many good poetry works, such as his series poems "Big Bombings "(大轰炸) reflecting NATO's Operation Allied Force in Kosovo, which published on Bulletin of Taiwanese Poetics in 1999.

Nowadays, Hong Kong is regarded as a cultural space with special properties such as marginalization and cross – border. As a relatively liberal literary port, it turns into the publishing and distributing public space for world Chinese literature (Yan, "The Different Narrative" 51). From the communication media perspective, literary journals have to practice worldwide idea well, and they need to face the challenges brought by the internet. Literature should achieve integrating between print media and network media. The development of Network culture drives forward rapidly and the shock wave brought by media network has begun to exclude traditional print media in Hong Kong. Books, as the carrier plane of literature in the past, also have gotten strong impact. Some literary sections of newspapers and magazines in websites, the click rate has exceeded their market sale. Besides, creating personal web page and blog are more and more prevalent, popular, thus a rather universal phenomenon on new literature in Hong Kong occurs: literature does not need to wait for the print publishing. People prefer to use the electronic transmission and directly list literature creating on web pages, in order to make more read and evaluate their work. This kind of network literature already attains in mainstream position and it will be the trend of Hong Kong literature remarked by critics. However, the biggest disadvantages of network literature lies in Hong Kong that works quality keeps large difference.

One of the reasons is lacking of the screening and proofreading process by network literature organizers (Chen, "Hronicle of Hong Kong's Literature" 13).

Although the historical situation of China including the social cultures of the
country are different from those in Western countries, its history of digitality and
electronic literature shows some parallel developments. The later development of
digitality and thus electronic literature itself happened in China owing to restrictions exerted on cultural industries and practices. However, once such restrictions were eased, digitality was embraced by the urban population and thus electronic literature too became an important activity. One distinction between Western and Chinese digital arts is the more collaborative ways practiced in China versus the more individual human – computer interaction created by Western artists.
While the theory and practice of Western electronic literature suggests that machines can get involved in the creation of literary texts, Chinese network literature has a bent towards the use of machines and technology in order to meet
people's communal needs. Regardless of cultural implications, new technologies
contribute to increase the interactive potential of art and literature. However,
Chinese critics of digitality and digital literature and art emphasize the fact that
meaningful interaction between human – machine interaction and the interpersonal
realm should be an objective (see, e. g. , Huang, "Toward a Digital Poetics"
102). Regarding the differences in literary genres between China and the West,
the poetic narrative remains the preferred textual format and dominant form of
digital literature in China, with Taiwan a leader in the e – poetry area. According to Ji Ma (马季), longer digital narratives can generally be divided into sev-
en types. The first type is the narration of changes in space – time locations with
people going back to a specific historical period and using their contemporary
knowledge to change the course of history. The second type is fantasy novels,
but that is different from Western science fiction. Western science fiction attaches importance to science basis; while Chinese network fantasy novel is not subject to the restriction of time and space or science, it's created freely by network
authors' unconstrained imaginary. The third refers to urban youth life describing

— 171 —

young people's emotions and their modern city life. Type four is about workplace struggles. The fifth type is adaptations of online computer games or other online material mostly for the purpose of marketing. The sixth type is the supernatural narrative depicting ghosts or adventure themes and thrillers. And the seventh type is military and martial arts (Ma, "Network Literature". People Daily, 19th, Apr., 2011).

In another perspective of explicating the Chinese development of digital literature, Mingfen Huang (黄鸣奋) suggests six characteristics of Chinese network literature: 1) the artist's identity is no longer the most important aspect of creativity and internet users acquire protagonist roles and use role play in their own work in order to inject emotion into the work; 2) just like the artist, the text is no longer an important aspects in cenarration develop by means of readers´participation in hypermedia; 3) traditional presentation and processes are no longer towards a fixed target and creation occurs by a complex combination of randomness and playfulness on the internet; 4) the audience is no longer silent, but participates actively with the digital text either by interacting with the text provided and/or by inputting their own contribution; 5) sources of the content of digital art are no longer "realist" (i. e., as in social realism), but "digital imagination", that is, the harmonious combination of art and activity, subjective and objective; and 6) the constructing factors for digital environments of art are not just between humans and nature, but including the machine and technical know – how (see "Toward a Digital Poetics"). In yet another perspective, network literature critic Hongbing Ge (葛红兵) uses three concepts to describe its characteristics: openness, quickness, and leisure and posits that if we admit that literature is a form of non – utilitarian "freedom" present within human nature, network literature is the best form to have the public experience this freedom in a multimodal form. He adds that one does not need elegance, mature technique, or high writing skills and that "immaturity" perhaps an advantage instead precisely because digital literature is unlike printed literature (74). Indeed, the rich and diverse contents of digital literature and the correspondingly large size of its user community has attracted the attention of many people in China and although this interest is at this time still concentrated in urban settings, there is no doubt that as China develops, also people in the countryside will engage with electronic literature especially because of the increase of handheld digital machines. This latter aspect is where China will undoubtedly advance faster than the West where digital interaction is more over "stationary" machines such as the computer and it remains to be seen whether in the West the use of the cell phone and similar handhelds would advance.

With regard to categories of users of digital literature it is interesting that dissimilar to the West, in China the male – female ratio of digital writers is almost equal, a factor that points to the active role of women in culture and the cultural industries. Writers come from diverse areas including some remote places, although the most popular ones tend to be in urban centers such as Beijing, Shanghai, Guangdong and similar. It is also important to mention that many writers do not come from the world of traditional art. Instead, they are amateur authors, civil servants, teachers, soldiers, workers, and even farmers who have technological knowledge. The creation of digital art happens like this: an author contributes a text to a discussion forum or online literature website and if it attracts readers and comments, it remains at the top of the discussion board and its popularity and value becomes widely recognized. A further "digitalization", as it were, occurs when the text in its original form or enhanced version (s) is adapted to film, a television play, computer games, etc. It can also occur that the text is published in printed form, that is, either as a traditional print book or as a digital book. This process includes the sudden rise of a writer out of obscurity or as a new writer and this emergence of an unknown writer would not happen in the traditional processes of established print culture.

It is because of the reach and possibilities of the digital that many established writers are using online discussion forums as their main avenue to increase the sale of their work, that is, the necessity to acquire readership and audience. Publishing houses engage in cooperation with websites to find, choose, and publish books. One consequence of this is that digital literature just like print literature now has top literature awards like the Xun Lu Literature Prize (鲁迅) or the Dun Mao Prize for Literature (矛盾). All this indicates that digital literature in China has become an important part of contemporary literature owing to its ways of the digital in creation, distribution and circulation, and users´ participation. While electronic literature in the West remains a specialized field, digital literature in China has changed the patterns of the literary system with regard to the production, distribution, reception, and post – processing of literary products. Compared with the high start – up costs of Western types of electronic literature, Chinese writers prefer to engage in a low – cost literary economy where it is more important to publish regularly in order to be in constant contact with one's readership.

The system differences between Western and Chinese digitality with regard to literary production I am referring to is observed by Hockx who writes thatthat vast majority of Chinese electronic literary production takes place in the context of millions of online discussion forums in thread format started by an author submitting a work (or a part of it) and extended by readers commenting and the author responding. Hockx also points out that the social community aspect of these sites prevents them from being considered innovative, avant – garde, or important in Western critical circles where the tradition and adherence to print culture determine that important works of electronic literature must be self – contained creations by individual and named creators. In China and possibly in other parts of the Chinese reading world as well, innovations are moving into a different direction employing the interactive features of digital online writing in order to produce unstable, multi – authored threads of writing and images which encourage participation and that involve their readership in new literary and aesthetic experiences. Further, on the one hand the communal aspect of the creation and consumption of digital literature makes one of communism's objectives— "public literature" — possible and fulfills the cooperative and democratic spirit of transferring literary discourse to the people. In addition, this results in the creation and development

of "新民间文学" ("new folk literature"), a particular genre that is by definition communal. But on the other hand, the limitations of digital literature in China are also obvious. Owing to the low threshold in both quality and cost, texts
pour into the internet without selection, so the government is beginning to take a
closer look at those productions. Huang conducted several surveys on the National
Library of China, as well as external institutions such as the Library of Congress
and the Widener Library at Harvard University and concludes that, in terms of
content, China produces more digital literature than any other country in the
world. However, compared with the research situation of electronic literature
worldwide, research into Chinese digital literature has serious shortcomings
(Huang, "Network Media Revolution" 61). There are several reasons for this:
one is that digital literature developed in China on the technical low – end because, initially, computer word processing and network transmission did not
support Chinese characters.

As I mention previously, it were Chinese students in the U. S. who created
Chinese character processing software and thus solved the problem of word processing in Chinese. Unfortunately, even with word processing technologies used
in digital literature, Western advances in digital writing techniques such as hy-
perlinks, multimedia content, the visualization of images, etc. , are rarely applied in Chinese digital literary creations. And Western high – end literary editing
systems and tools such as "Story Space" and "Super Card Editor" are not recommended or modified for creative online writings in Chinese. Online digital texts in
China are produced merely by the simple process of using the Chinese character
input method with content originally written on paper and transmitted to the internet in the traditional linear manner (on this, see Shan, "Falseness of the
'Fad'"). Thus, over the past twenty years, the development of digital literature in China belongs to low – technical digital creation with the exception of a
few hypertext writings. This is one of the reasons why scholarship and the critical
evaluation of digital literature in Chinese is yet to develop. Of course, there is
also the opinion by some, even influential, scholars and writers that in principle

there is no difference between a text printed and a text created and published digitally: clearly, such opinion lacks the perspective of the interactive nature of digital literature and the different function of readership. A similar situation is the case with regard to digital humanities, a recently developed field in which the theory and practice of digital literature can be located (for a bibliography of work in the field see Tötösy de Zepetnek < http: //docs. lib. purdue. edu/clcweblibrary/bibliographydigitalhumanities >).

As I suggest above, the designation "network literature" includes the publishing of not only electronic literature, but all sorts of digital texts and this means that also the publishing of scholarship belongs to "network literature. " Similar to the U. S. and Europe, the acceptance of humanities scholarship published online is slow in China because of the academic world's cautious adaptation of publishing online and even the employment of new media in pedagogy (on this, see, e. g. , Tötösy de Zepetnek and Jia < http: //dx. doi. org/10. 7771/ 1481 – 4374. 2426 > ; Tötösy de Zepetnek and Boruszko < http: //stateofthediscipline. acla. org/entry/paradigm – shift – comparative – humanities – digital – humanities – pedagogy – new – media – technology – and >). Another issue is with regard to the acceptance and award of credit for online publications because there are few online only journals which are also Thomson Reuters indexed, the latter of which being an absolute requirement in China and Taiwan (also in India and Europe, but not in the U. S. and Canada) for receiving credit for a publication.

In conclusion, the development of digital media and internet – based communication have brought about huge transformations in Chinese literature and resulted in fundamental changes in the aesthetic structures, various concepts of literature, and the production and reception of literature. Using the narrative style of ordinary people has prompted literature to turn towards a new kind of folk writing style with few restrictions on the canon and more freedom for popular art. The other side of the coin is that, for some critics, technology may destroy some of the humanist characteristics which where part of art and literature for centuries and reduce the ethical responsibility of the artist/writer towards his/her community of readers. Chinese cultural industries struggle to retain this original humanist spirit without falling into the demands of the market and profitability. As Ouyang points out, the Chinese literary scene needs to balance artistic reliance on technology with a certain degree of self – discipline and community spirit in order to become a real and effective driver of Chinese cultural representations globally (Ouyang, "Digital Media": 143).

REFERENCES

[1] Book Sina (新浪读书频道) <http://book.sina.com.cn/>

[2] Chen shaohua (陈少华). 香港文学十年志 (hronicle of Hong kong's Literature in the Past Decade) [J]. Taiwan, Hong Kong and Overseas Chinese Literature 3 2007 (3): 6 – 17.

[3] China News Digest (华夏文摘) <http://www.cnd.org/whatiscnd.html>

[4] China Internet Network Information Center. China Internet Network Development Statistical Report (中国互联网络发展状况统计报告) [M]. 2015: 1 – 128.

[5] Chinese All (中文在线) <http://www1.chineseall.com>

[6] *Cloudary.com.cn* (盛大文学网官网) <http://www.cloudary.com.cn/introduce.html>.

[7] *Electronic Literature Directory* (2014): <http://directory.eliterature.org/>

[8] Energy – saving (红袖添香) <http://www.hongxiu.com/>

[9] Ge Hongbing (葛红兵). 网络文学: 新世纪文学新生的可能性 ("Network Literature: The Possibility of the Revitalization of Literature in a New Age"). Social Sciences, 2001 (8): 73 – 74.

[10] Gu Yuanqing (古远清). 香港文学研究 20 年 (Hong Kong literature Research for the past Twenty Years) [J]. Academic Research, (2002) (7): 112 – 16.

[11] Hockx Michel. Internet Literature in China [M]. New York: Columbia UP, 2015.

[12] Huang Mingfen (黄鸣奋). 网络传媒革命与电子文学批评的嬗变 ([M] Network Media Revolution and Evolution of Electronic Literary Criticism) [J]. Exploration and Free Views, 11 2010 (11): 58 – 62.

[13] Huang Mingfen（黄鸣奋）. 从电子文学、网络文学到数码诗学：理论创新的呼唤（Toward a Digital Poetics for Electronic and Internet Literature）［J］. Theoretical Studies in Literature and Art, 2014 (1)：99 - 105.

[14] Hsiu Wen - wei（须文蔚）. 台湾数位文学论（On Taiwan's Digital Literature Theory）［J］. Taipei：2 - fishes Culture, 2003.

[15] Jinjiang City Literature（晋江文学城）< http：//www. jjwxc. net/ >

[16] Lin Qiyang（林淇瀁）. 书写与拼图—台湾文学传播现象研究（Writing and Jigsaw：On the Phenomenon of Literature Communication in Taiwan）［J］. Taipei：Rye Field Publishing, 2001.

[17] Li Qingben（李庆本）. Beijing as a World City：An Exploration of Its Cultural and Creative Industries. ［M］//Cityscapes：World Cities and Their Cultural Industries. Ed. Asunción López - Varela. Champaign：Common Ground Publishing, 2013：1 - 12.

[18] Ma Ji（马季）. 网络文学：中国当代文学第二次起航（Network Literature：The Second Sailing of Chinese Contemporary Literature）［J］. People Daily, 2011 (4).

[19] Miall David S. Representing and Interpreting Literature by Computer ［J］. Yearbook of English Studies, 1995 (25)：199 - 212.

[20] New Threads（新语丝）< http：//www. xys. org >

[21] Ouyang Youquan（欧阳有权）. 网络文学概论（Introduction to Network Literature）［M］. Beijing：Peking UP, 2007.

[22] Ouyang Youquan（欧阳有权）. 新世纪以来网络文学研究综述（Research on Network Literature in China in New Century）［J］. Modern Literary Magazine, 2007 (1)：451 - 54.

[23] Ouyang Youquan（欧阳有权）. 网络文学本体论纲（Outline of the Ontology of Network Literature）［J］. Literary Review, 2004 (6)：69 - 74.

[24] Ouyang Youquan（欧阳有权）. 数字媒介与中国文学的转型（Digital Media and Transformation of Chinese Literature）［J］. Social Science in China, 2007 (1)：143 - 56.

[25] Rongshu Xia（榕树下）< http：//www. rongshuxia. com >

[26] Shan Xiaoxi（单晓曦）. "改编热" 的虚妄与数字文学性的开掘—评网络文学的影视剧改编现象及其发展路向（Falseness of the "Fad" of Arrangement and Digging of Digital Literariness：A Comment on the Phenomenon and Development of Film and Television Arrangements in Network Literature）［J］. Arts Criticism, 2012 (5)：75 - 80.

[27] Shi jianwei（施建伟）. 世界华文文学中的香港文学（Hong Kong Literature in global

Chinese Literature）［J］. Journal of Tongji University（social science section），1999
(3)：62 - 66.

［28］ Start Chinese Net（起点中文网）< http：//top. qidian. com/ >

［29］ The Garden of Forking Paths（岐路花园）< http：//benz. nchu. edu. tw/ ~ garden/a -
works. htm >

［30］ Tötösy de Zepetnek Steven. Bibliography for Work in Digital Humanities and（Inter）
mediality Studies［J］. Library Series，CLCWeb：Comparative Literature and Culture
(2013 -)：< http：//docs. lib. purdue. edu/clcweblibrary/bibliographydigitalhumani-
ties >

［31］ Vuillemin Alain and Michel Lenoble. Littératureetinformatique［J］. LaLittératuregénérée
par ordinateur. Arras：Artois PU，1995.

［32］ Wang Xiaofei's（王 笑 飞）Chinese Poetry. website：< chpoem - 1 @
listserv. acsu. buffalo. edu >.

［33］ Wei Yagui's（魏亚桂）network newsgroup < alt. chinese. text >.

［34］ Xiangyang Workshop（向阳工坊）< http：//hylim. myweb. hinet. net/ >.

［35］ Xiangyang Poetry Space（向阳诗房）< http：//tea. ntue. edu. tw/ ~ xiangyang/xian-
gyang/ >.

［36］ Xiangyang Literary World（向阳文苑）< http：//tns. ndhu. edu. tw/ ~ xiangyang/in-
dex. htm >.

［37］ Xiangyang. A Torn Poem（一首被撕裂的诗）. < http：//tea. ntue. edu. tw/ ~ xiangy-
ang/workshop/netpoetry/ >.

［38］ Yan. min（颜敏）.“世界性”的差异表述—1980 年代以来中国内地、新马和中国
香港文学期刊的华文文学传播（The Different Narrative of Cosmopolitan：A Study on
the Communication of HuaWen Literature in the Literary Journals of the Mainland of Chi-
na，Singapore and Malaysia and Hong Kong since 1980）［J］. Journal of Guangdong
University of Education，2012（4）：47 - 54.

Conclusions

Nowadays, the process of globalization continues to develop, and cross-cultural communication has become more frequent in the whole world. In the 1990s, Joseph Nye, American scholar and professor at Harvard University, firstly proposed the Theory of Soft Power in his book *Bound to Lead: the Changing Nature of American Power*. He pointed out that a comprehensive national strength of a country both include "hard power" represented by economy, science technology, military strength performance, and the "soft power" embodied in cultural and ideological attractiveness. Hard power and soft power are still important, but in the Information Age, soft power is becoming more prominent than ever. (Joseph Nye, 1990)

Cultural soft power is a concept derived from the theory of Soft Power, and a strength based on cultural resources. In the current era of globalization, the importance and urgency of constructing cultural soft power are particularly prominent. However, all cultures of a country do not mean all its soft power. "When one country's cultural products are received by other countries or nations, presenting positive impacts, this kind can be regarded as cultural soft power (Hujian, 2011). As China's most profound elements of cultural soft power, Chinese traditional culture has the characteristic of "harmony" as the core. In the current era of multicultural globalization, it coruscates the appeal and charming of Chinese culture. The core of constructing Chinese cultural soft power is to carry forward excellent part of Chinese traditional culture, to make Chinese culture effectively "go out", and "walk in ". Therefore, it is an important task for China to enhance the image of the country and the speaking right in international stage by carrying forward Chinese culture and promote its integration in the world.

There are at least two ways by means of which national culture can become international: in translation and in cross – cultural adaptation. Translation is not only the conversion of language, but also the selection and cultural variations through adaptation. As indicated, it is important to point out that cross – cultural variations are not just unidirectional but multidirectional, that is, cultural intersections take place across space and time. However, if some meanings are laid beyond the language of text, which translation can't express, the further full explanations will be needed.

This volume has focused on cross – cultural semiotics interpretations exploring issues of language and various other forms of cultural representation in order to rethink worldwide relationships. The multi – dimensional model of cross – cultural research presented in the book defends a temporal semiotic orientation, rather than a purely spatial approach for intercultural interpretation. The volume insists that in the age of globalization, cultural identity is unavoidably a very sharp question, and that multiple layers of meanings are involved in cultural identity. Thus, it explores differences and parallelisms between Western and Chinese semiotics, conservative and as well as unconventional approaches – misappropriation, transplantation, transfer and transformation—in Chinese aesthetics in different media. For example, adaptations are contemplated as intercultural avenues for learning about the West and exporting Chinese culture to the world, showing the complexity of cross – cultural exchanges. which are never merely one – directional and which include temporal mappings. In the case of one of the dramas explored in this volume, *The Orphan of Zhao* by Ji Junxiang (纪君祥), the journey is from ancient Chinese culture to Western culture, and then back to modern Chinese culture. In the case of Shakespeare's adaptations, other patterns are explored in order to show how the bard's dramas are staged and interpreted by Chinese audiences.

An underlying topic in the volume is the exploration of how the national becomes international, and how certain literary representations and adaptations become World Literature, read and understood by the readers of other cultures because it has features that transcend the specificity of a given nation. The volume ends of a look at China's rapid development in technological changes and its impact upon intermedial practices. Focusing drama, cinema and electronic literature, the multidirectional cross – cultural approach presented here seeks to provide avenues for intercultural dialogue in a globalized world.

REFERENCES

Joseph S. Nye Jr. *Bound to Lead: The Changing Nature of American Power*, Basic Books Press, 1991.